YOU BET YOUR GARDEN® GUIDE TO

GROWING GREAT
Tomatoes

SECOND EDITION

YOU BET YOUR GARDEN® GUIDE TO

GROWING GREAT

SECOND EDITION

Tomatoes

How to Grow Great-Tasting Tomatoes in Any Backyard, Garden, or Container

Mike McGrath

FOX CHAPEL
PUBLISHING

© 2002, 2009, 2012, 2020 by Mike McGrath.
Illustrations © 2002, 2009, 2012, 2020 by Signe Wilkinson.
Photography © Gurney's Seed & Nursery Company (Gurneys.com) except as noted.

You Bet Your Garden® is a registered trademark of Mike McGrath Enterprises, Inc.

First published in 2002 as *You Bet Your Tomatoes!* by Rodale Books.
Second edition published in 2009 as *You Bet Your Tomatoes!* by Plain White Press.
New revised and expanded editions published in 2012 and 2020 as *You Bet Your Garden Guide to Growing Great Tomatoes* by Fox Chapel Publishing Company, Inc., 903 Square Street, Mount Joy, PA 17552.

The author and publisher wish to express their thanks and appreciation to Gurney's Seed & Nursery Company (*Gurneys. com*) for their assistance and generosity in providing the color photos of tomatoes for the 2012 and 2020 editions. Unless otherwise noted, all photos are provided by Gurney's © 2012, 2020. Used with permission. All rights reserved. Additional photo credits found on page 120.

ISBN 978-1-4971-0075-6

Library of Congress Control Number:2019950557

To learn more about the other great books from Fox Chapel Publishing, or to find a retailer near you, call toll-free 800-457-9112 or visit us at *www.FoxChapelPublishing.com*.

We are always looking for talented authors. To submit an idea, please send a brief inquiry to acquisitions@foxchapelpublishing.com.

Printed in Singapore
First printing

Because working with gardening equipment and other materials inherently includes the risk of injury and damage, this book cannot guarantee that creating the projects in this book is safe for everyone. For this reason, this book is sold without warranties or guarantees of any kind, expressed or implied, and the publisher and the author disclaim any liability for any injuries, losses, or damages caused in any way by the content of this book or the reader's use of the tools needed to complete the projects presented here. The publisher and the author urge all readers to thoroughly review each project and to understand the use of all tools before beginning any project.

Foreword to the *New New New* Edition

Welcome to the newest edition of *You Bet Your Tomatoes!*, now titled *You Bet Your Garden® Guide to Growing Great Tomatoes*.

A lot of wonderful things have happened to this humble gardener in the years since the earliest edition of this tome was first published by Rodale Books (where I was privileged to serve as Editor-in-Chief of *Organic Gardening* for seven years—sixty issues of the world's greatest gardening magazine!—in the 1990s). My public radio show, *You Bet Your Garden®*, which debuted in October 1998, was just going national as the first edition of the book went to press. Now, more than two decades (and many hundreds of shows) later, this hour of horticultural hijinks can be heard on public radio stations around the country, as an Internet stream, and even as a podcast (with over one million listeners a year— thank you!). There's even a TV show! Find out more by visiting *www.YouBetYourGarden.org*.

Thanks to the show, I've had the opportunity over the years to add to my storehouse of tomato-growing knowledge (and other organic information) via the Question of the Week feature, in which I provide a detailed explanation of a particular problem or gardening topic at the *You Bet Your Garden®* section of the Gardens Alive! website (*www.GardensAlive.com*). There, you'll find even *more* tomato-growing advice (who would have thought it possible?!), like how to handle

Author Mike McGrath.

squirrels, stink bugs, squirrels, and other specific pests and problems (like squirrels). And don't just hang around the tomato section; wander afar and afield and you'll find organic answers to virtually every garden and home problem that may have otherwise tempted you to spray away.

We have once again completely revisited, revamped, and updated our tomato-growing information and top varieties, making everything as current and up-to-date as possible at the time of printing to bring you even more information about America's favorite fruit (or, as I like to call it, "the Gateway Drug of Gardening").

See you on the radio. Or TV (do any of you still watch TV?). Podcast! I know we got you hooked on the podcast. I won't actually "see" you there (this ain't *Romper Room* [at least most of the time]), but I'll know you're listening.

Well—not really. Read the book, OK?

Mike McGrath

Mike McG, canning a record amount of sauce in the summer of 2019

Contents

Introduction

Why Am I Doing *This* instead of Enjoying My Summer?

Sooner or later, anyone who claims to be a gardener (or Italian) has to grow his own fresh, vine-ripened summer tomatoes. Resistance is futile, so you might as well accept the inevitable and start staggering around the garden getting it ready for you to put your tomatoes in nice and early this season (that way you might end up with some actual *ripe* ones before hard frost comes a-knocking).

Like other things you might possibly have no actual interest in achieving and/or live in abject fear of (like climbing a big frozen mountain or buying a minivan), if you claim the gardening mantle, you *must* grow tomatoes "because they are there." Well, actually they *aren't* there yet. But they sure will be there once you get growing, won't they? You hope.

Anyway, there are lots of neat *actual* reasons why you should grow your own tomatoes.

Here are just a few:

- All of the tomatoes for sale in grocery stores are genetically engineered with DNA taken from Alex Trebek, Wink Martindale, Whoopi Goldberg, Pat Sajak, or some other game-show type when he wasn't paying attention.
- You can't afford a boat, but still have a desperate need to show your neighbors you know how to foolishly waste your time and money in a really pointless manner.
- They're easier to grow than watermelons…
- …and it's a *lot* easier to tell when they're ripe.
- Most other summertime endeavors have a much higher risk of death and/or dismemberment.

> Everyone grows their tomatoes in the summer—unless they live in Arizona, southern Texas, or some other place so hot they have to grow their tomatoes over the winter and live in deep holes in the sand all summer to escape the heat.

Cupid

The lady's name is **Cupid.** Pretty cute, eh? But is the fruit of this romantically named variety meant to look like a little Valentine heart? Or the part of everyone's favorite cherub archer's anatomy you see as he's flying away from you?

- You'll have a handy excuse for avoiding those treacherous family reunion picnics, mosquito- and blackfly-infested hikes, frolics in freezing cold ocean waves, and other festive seasonal outings you'd be dragged to if you couldn't say, "Gee, I'd love to go, but I performed a biodynamic copper flange pruning on my tomato plants last night, and I have to stay here and spray them with compost tea that was fermented in a ram's horn under a full moon, or the pistils won't be firm."
- You'll be able to throw around gardening terms like "pistil" and "compost tea" without being laughed at…maybe.
- There's probably something even more tedious you'd have to do *inside* the house if you didn't have the tomatoes to herd.
- You'll have a great reason (OK, *"excuse"*, but it's your word against theirs) to buy, rent, or borrow a big tiller and thus use a really noisy, dangerous piece of gasoline-powered equipment.
- You can wait until those annoying neighbors (oh, come on—you know *exactly* who I mean) have company over in their oh-so-perfect backyard to fire up that really noisy piece of power equipment.
- You'll be able to cut the family food bill by a good thirty or forty dollars a year—while spending less than the cost of a new car to grow your own tomatoes!
- When your kids complain that they're bored for the 368th time during the summer (and school's only been out for a month), you can say, "Well, you could always weed the tomatoes."

But seriously, folks, there is one big, overwhelming reason you really *should* grow your own tomatoes:

1) There is honestly nothing that can compare to the taste of a fresh, vine-ripened tomato, plucked at the perfect peak of sweetness and eaten warm and sugary, tart and juicy, right there in the garden as you make a big mess all over your shirt.

2) If you actually get good at this (and you can—I grow *great* tomatoes just about every season, and I barely have opposable thumbs), you'll have access to the ultimate summertime bragging right: "Oh, and would you like a slice of fresh tomato on that? Let me go out and pick a nice one for you."

3) If you get really good at it, you can go for the gold: Having ripe, red tomatoes conspicuously hanging on your plants *days* before that pain-in-the-butt gardener down the block who's been showing off for years.

4) And then nirvana: Knocking on that gardener's door with a bag of ripe tomatoes while *his* first love apples are still green and saying, "Here—I noticed your plants don't seem to be doing very well this year, and we've had more than we can eat for weeks now…"

5) Start your own tomatoes from seed, and you can grow (and share and savor and *really* brag about) wonderful varieties that you just can't find already started for you at the garden center, much less the supermarket, like Tigerella, Brandywine, Big Rainbow, Radiator Charlie's Mortgage Lifter…

Well, yes, that's actually *five* reasons. And yes, I *did* begin by writing that "there is one big overwhelming reason you should grow your own…" I thought you should know that you're about to take gardening advice from a man who can't count. To one.

Here is a nice example of my personal favorite type of tomato: a large beefsteak that begins life green, ripens to yellow, and then continues ripening to develop red streaks throughout the fruit (making the sliced fruit look like a frozen sunset!). Many named varieties sport this size and impressive color combination, including Striped Marvel (aka Marvel Striped), Big Rainbow, and Georgia Streak. With a great mix of sweetness and acidity, this is a must try tomato type for those with room to grow big plants.

Chapter 1

"Picking" Your Tomatoes

. . . .

(Do all of these things have funny, rude, or mysterious names?)

There are no "wrong" tomatoes (other than those waxed-fruit varieties in the supermarket); you should grow what you like. So I'll provide a few basic facts and helpful information—like how to start the seeds, how to support the plants, and how long you generally have to wait for ripe tomatoes—and *you* will fall in love with weird names and romantic illusions and grow as many different *solanaceous* flights of fancy as you can. Some will become your tomatoes forever, while others will end up being a dimly recalled one-season stand. That's OK—you're young and foolish, and we don't judge. (Unless you dismiss the flavor of a first-rate tomato like big juicy Brandywine as "mealy" or something.)

Anyway, tomatoes are like wine—because all the good ones are red! (White wine is something you drink when you're sick, like tea.) Actually, unlike wine, some of the best tomatoes aren't red (but they aren't white either, tea drinker!). Seriously, tomatoes really *are* like wine—because you often have the most fun when you break the rules.

Jet Star

Jet Star is a hybrid variety with a reputation for extremely high sugar content, massive production, and rampant vine growth—so give this candy factory lots of room. Said to do well even in cool climes, Jet Star is a real favorite of fresh eaters who have a Love Apple Sweet Tooth.

The wild world of heirlooms! Crazy colors, weird shapes, and the kinds of flavor that true tomato growers crave. Don't worry about a few "cracks" here and there, because these are the Real Deal!

These almost-a-beefsteak-but-not-quite tomatoes are clearly growing on an indeterminate plant. Pick them promptly (the one on the bottom left is ready to come inside), because prompt picking encourages the plant to keep producing.

Sometimes this "there are two types of…" thing gets out of hand. My favorite is, "There are two types of people—those who break society down into two types of people, and those who don't." I attribute this to Oscar Wilde but might have read it in a comic book.

What's Your Tomato Determination?

There are two main types of tomato plants, and the difference is important.

Determinate. Determinate plants pretty much stop growing around the time the bulk of their tomatoes form, producing almost all of their potential fruit in that one big flush. Then, they are mostly done for the season. Obviously such plants are great for large-scale farming, but they're also good for gardeners (like *moi*) who cook down a lot of their crop to jar up as sauce and paste for the winter: You can pick enough tomatoes from one or two determinate plants in a couple of days to make a full pot of sauce, cook it up, and be done instead of making small batches all the time. That's probably why most—but not all—paste tomatoes are determinate. Determinate plants also tend to be smaller and more compact, making them good choices for small-space and container gardens. And determinate varieties move in and out of your garden *fast*, allowing you to pull up those plants when they're done producing and replace them with garlic, lettuce, spinach, broccoli, and/or other fall-planted crops. (Which you *should* do—every space in your kitchen garden should produce at least two different runs of edibles.)

Indeterminate. Indeterminate plants grow like big honking teenagers you *just* bought new clothes for. Their vines don't stop creeping toward the next county until they're killed by frost (although they'll slow down quite a bit when the days get shorter and the nights get cooler). Indeterminates produce flowers and fruit sequentially throughout the season, making them great choices for folks who simply want to enjoy a nice steady supply of fresh tomatoes all summer long. Just be aware that indeterminate plants tend to be large and sprawling—the opposite of compact.

Most of the old, great-tasting heirloom varieties—and big tomatoes in general—are indeterminate. The yield on some indeterminate plants is sometimes smaller than that of the more compact varieties, but sometimes their extended tomato production time evens things out over the course of a season. And big tomatoes like the treasured heirloom varieties *need* a larger leaf-to-fruit ratio to create their bigger, much more complex flavors, and so more of the plant's energy has to go into making solar-collecting leaves to feed those highly anticipated fruits. As with wine grapes, the smaller the harvest, the more intense the flavor of the fruits.

Note: You may see some varieties listed as *semi-determinate* or described using similar weasel words. This means:

1) You can expect this variety to have some of each characteristic, maybe producing most of its tomatoes in a big flush, but on vines longer than a determinate; or (you wish), a big honkin' variety whose vines are somewhat better behaved than the norm.

And:

2) Nobody really knows, and this way you can't complain when what was supposed to be a cute little tomato shoves your pepper plants into the street.

More Stuff to Think About

Now that you've *determined* which type you most want to grow, you'll probably want to lie down and rest for awhile. Too bad! Tomato growing isn't for wimps, and you're not done yet; there are other seed catalog variables you'll want to consider before making your choices.

DAYS TO MATURITY (DTM)

You should see a specific number of days listed on every packet of seed, included in the description of each tomato variety in seed catalogs, and, if you're lucky, on those little plant tags stuck in the dirt of garden center transplants. An intelligent person might presume it refers to the average number of days it will take before you bite into your first ripe tomato, which would be correct for a plant you buy already started at the garden center, but a damned lie for the seed packet and/or catalog, because it is *actually* the number of days it will take the average *six-week-old transplant* to produce edible fruit. So for plants you start from seed, you would add fifty or sixty days of anxious anticipation to that number. (The extra time is for the seeds to germinate and for the always necessary Wiggle Room.)

….Hmmm. You know, by *law*, these numbers only *have* to be found *on* seed packets, so why should *we* have to do the math?

Oh well, DTMs are very useful numbers, *especially* if you live in a frequently frozen latitude. A short growing season means you should stick with tomatoes with the lowest DTMs, even if you intend to start them early, protect them with special warming things like cloches, row covers, or Wall-O-Waters early in the season, and so forth. And yes, the

Seed packets (and plant tags) may or may not reveal the determination of a tomato, but most *will* have a DTM (days to maturity) number on the seed packet and/or plant tag. That's the number of days on average that will pass after you put a six- to eight-week-old transplant in the ground before you can expect to pick your first ripe tomato—no matter how much you encourage and/or threaten the plant.

corollary is also true; if you have a *long* season, *do* look for big numbers. Take advantage of what some of us *don't* have—lots of growing days—and enjoy the rarest and best-tasting heirlooms, some of which can take what seems like *forever* to produce their first ripe fruit.

Otherwise, plant as many different kinds of tomatoes as you can fit into your garden space: beefsteaks, slicers, oxhearts, heirlooms, patios, plums, pears, cherries…!

Before we move on, though, let's get into DTMs in a bit more detail. Really short DTMers like Early Girl and Stupice (named after me) can produce ripe love apples in 50 or so days. They ain't the best tasting, but they're there. (Insert Cheech and Chong joke here. Or right there on the side of this page works too.)

On the other end of the scale, some big honking heirlooms can take up to 90 or 100 days. Do the math. Oh, OK, I'll do it: The math says you better have enough time in the growing season where you live.

DTMs under 70 will almost always be determinate varieties that produce most of their fruits within a tight span of a few days and then *maybe* a few more over the course of the season, but not enough to justify their garden footprint. Farmers love this. They can circle a date 55 days from planting big, healthy starts, schedule the picking, and then be ready to plant the follow-up crop, like string beans or garlic. Most home gardeners with a single plant in the ground, though, were not hoping for twenty pounds of fruit on Thursday.

Your options if you have an avalanche of tomatoes on the aforementioned Thursday:

- Make tomato sauce early. Many—if not most—"early" varieties were bred for processing. If it's *damn* hot (as opposed to just hot), do it on that side burner on your outdoor grill.
- Keep an eye on your neighbor's gardens. If they're growing big honking heirlooms, they'll be lucky to have flowers, much less greenies, when *your* crop comes in. Put six of your nicest-looking dead-ripe red love apples in a brown paper lunch bag, wait for your neighbors to pull into their driveway, and walk over with your gift. "We've noticed your tomatoes don't seem to be doing too well, and we have more than we can use…" (Philadelphia note: "It is not enough to succeed; others must fail.")

Otherwise, you will wait until mid-August (in the Mid-Atlantic and North) for the big heirloom beefsteaks to ripen up. (Actually, they'll still be green; just wanted you to feel better/worse). Do the math,

Obligatory Cheech and Chong joke:

Q: "Hey man—how good is it?"

A: "It's here; that makes it great."

Super Sweet 100

Super Sweet 100 is an improved (more disease-resistant) variety of the classic Sweet 100 cherry tomato. There is also a further improved (and downright inflationary!) version known as Sweet Million, bred to produce larger fruit.

Kookie—add 90 days to June 1st (it was a cold spring) and whaddya get? At least those brats of yours are back in school.

Bottom line: Nobody wants 20 pounds of tamatas on the 10th of July. And nobody wants to wait until the heat comes back on in the house for their first tamata. So what do you do?

You play the DTM game with 1960s rock 'n' roll tomato planting! Let's say you have room for eight tomato plants. Make two of them the earliest varieties possible—like Fourth of July, Stupice, Early Girl… These are the opening acts. Think Aztec Two-Step, Brewer & Shipley, Tommy James & the Shondells.

The next two are rated around 70 days; they're bigger and tastier. We're talking Joan Jett, Genya Ravan, Mason Willmans, and John Prine.

Next up splits the difference. With DTMs of 80 to 90, you're in a better zone than most home gardeners can imagine. This is Deep Purple (which should be a real tomato name), Ultimate Spinach (a real band name; look it up), Strawberry Alarm Clock (ibid.) and/or the Cowsills (the name of your favorite song by them is not "The Flower Girl," it's "The Rain, the Park, and Everything" [don't blame me; I would have voted for "The Flower Girl"…]).

And then, ladies and gentlemen, our featured performers—The Rolling Stonies, The Who, Paul McWhereami?, Pink Floyd (which really should be a variety name!). That's right—the headliners! The best-tasting and most gifted guitar-playing tomatoes of them all! Who cares that the back-to-school stuff is now on closeout at Wally World—you are now enjoying *the* best tomatoes in all of whatever-dom, *after* enjoying the opening acts for the previous two months.

Give it up for DTMs!

"Thank you; thank you very much."

"Brandywine has now left the building. If you're driving home tonight, be sure you have a car."

TYPES

You've got your huge beefsteaks, your tidy little pasters, your sweet, invasive little cherries (a.k.a. weeds), your romantic (kind of) looking oxhearts, and your regular round slicing/salad tomatoes. If you've got the room, grow at least one of each type you can come up with—and don't be didactic about how you use them. Beefsteak types can be great for processing; they add a *lot* of distinctive tomato flavor to the finished sauce. And many folks *prefer* to use meaty paste tomatoes on sandwiches—there's a lot less messy juice to make the bread all soggy.

However, *don't* grow cherry tomatoes unless you:
a) have *lots* of room (they can make pumpkin vines look tentative);
b) grow for fresh eating (how many cherry tomatoes *would* it take to make a pint of sauce? You stand a better chance of guessing the number of pennies in those water-tower-sized jars at county fairs);
c) don't mind bazillions of volunteer cherry tomato plants coming up in your garden for decades to come; and
d) have *lots* of room.

OK—if you love popping the little treats in your mouth, but are short on space, try to find one of the determinate varieties of cherry tomatoes—they're not such terrible space hogs. But their reseeding habit is still as invasive as kudzu.

Perhaps the best way to grow cherry tomatoes is in *big* hanging baskets. That way, they're not taking up valuable garden space, and they're not crawling on the ground where slugs and mice will wreak havoc on them and where they'll drop that endless seed we just spoke of. And if you hang them properly, you can just stagger outside, pop as many into your mouth as you want—*without bending over* (YBYG rule #3: "Bending is for chumps")—and then run back into the air conditioning.

The bigger the container, the better. It should be made of solid plastic; otherwise the watering will become more tedious than riding in an elevator where a child too small for you to slap has pressed all the buttons while the parents stare blankly into space. The bigger the container, the less often you will need to water. The more inert the container (e.g., hard plastic), the less often you will need to water. Really cool-looking containers made of terra cotta will need to be watered daily. Really *really* cool-looking containers made of peat moss or coir (shredded coconut husks) will need to be watered hourly. Unless it's *extremely* hot out, and then you're just screwed.

OPEN-POLLINATED OR HYBRID: SCIENCE TIME!

Essentially, the difference here is that if you save seeds from the fruit of an *open-pollinated* variety (such as Brandywine) and plant those seeds the following year, those seeds will grow you the same type of plant with the same kind of fruit (in this case, big tasty Brandywines).

Hybrids are the product of a deliberate mating of two different varieties in order to combine two desirable characteristics—like, for instance, to get some improved disease resistance into a very tasty,

Hybridizing is *not* genetic engineering, by the way, where a modern day Colin Clive inserts a fish gene into a tomato to make it swim better. (Colin Clive played Dr. Frankenstein—It's alive! Alive! Hahahaha!—in the original Boris Karloff movies. Sadly, his tomato preferences are unknown.)

but disease-prone, variety of tomato. The process of creating hybrid seed is fairly complex and very labor-intensive. Basically, you force the flowers of two different, carefully chosen plants to have sex with each other, then protect the resulting pollinated flowers from any outside interference, like bees or wind (usually by covering the newly-pollinated flowers with paper bags). The seeds taken from the fruit that results will produce offspring that are different from either of the parents (like those bratty kids of yours).

The growers and sellers of hybrid seeds have to do this fresh each season—combining the pollen of those same two different varieties every year to create (actually, re-create) the hybrid variety. If you grow a hybrid tomato from seed or started plants, you will get the hybrid plant and fruit, with all of the traits the hybridization was designed to achieve. But if you *save the seeds* from some of your hybrid tomatoes and plant them the following season, you will *not* get those same improved plants or fruit. You *will* get tomato plants of some kind, but they might not be very good ones.

By law, hybrid plants and seeds must be identified by the word "hybrid" or the term "f1."

Some hard-line organic folks oppose hybrids on the grounds that they're not "natural" plants, but there's nothing diabolical—or even bad—about the process, and it has *nothing* to do with gene-jerking around. Professionals and talented amateurs have been hybridizing plants for centuries. (Heck—it evens happens out in nature, when frisky bees get promiscuous with different plants in the same genus.) I don't personally have a problem with hybrid varieties and have grown many hybrids in my own garden. And some folks—in challenging climates and/or areas with extreme disease pressures, for instance—can really use the specialized traits of some hybrids as insurance against the awful possibility of a—*sob*—tomato-free summer.

And most of the varieties that have been *proven* to be resistant to specific diseases and pests are hybrids. So go ahead and grow a few if you like—just don't save the seeds to start next year's crop.

Now, let's move on to some of your best choices. Organized by type (beefsteak, paster, etc.).

ONE MORE DEFINITION: HEIRLOOMS!

"Heirloom" tomatoes are at the root of tomato gardening. The best definition of an heirloom variety is a tomato that was once available commercially (in, say, a 1910 or 1911 seed catalog), but was discontinued, became *un*available in the seed trade, and only survives today thanks to dedicated home gardeners. These enthusiasts *loved* the specific variety in question, and saved some seeds from their best tomatoes season after season so they could continue to grow them, often because they were unique in some way: flavor, color (some *wild* ones), size, disease resistance, productivity, etc. By definition, therefore, all heirlooms are open-pollinated varieties. Thanks to a renaissance in old-time tomato interest—and the fine work of the individuals and organizations that have tracked down the descendants of the original savers who were still growing out and saving the seeds—many of these great varieties are once again available to all.

This tomato shows the classic **"beefsteak"** shape, prized by those who want a single tomato slice to cover a sandwich—and maybe hang over the edges a little. It's available under its generic name ("beefsteak," which has become more of a type over the years than a single variety name) and also has many more intricately named varieties. All are classic "bragging" tomatoes thanks to their size, flavor, and deep red color.

Top Tomatoes
BEEFSTEAKS AND SLICERS

© tomatofest.com

Arkansas Traveler

Indeterminate	Open-pollinated	89 days to maturity

Comments

Legendary pink heirloom; can handle hot and dry climates; good in South. *Proven* to be resistant to specific diseases and/or pests.

Big Beef

Indeterminate	Hybrid	73 days to maturity

Comments

One of the best producers of really huge tomatoes; old-time tomato flavor. *Observed* to be resistant to specific diseases and/or pests.

Photo by David Cavagnaro.

Big Boy

Indeterminate	Open-pollinated	78 days to maturity

Comments

Thick-walled, meaty one-pounders (450g).

Big Rainbow

Indeterminate	Open-pollinated	100 days to maturity

Comments

Huge, beautiful, tasty heirloom; red streaks through gold fruit; takes heat well. *Proven* to be resistant to specific diseases and/or pests.

Black Krim

Indeterminate	Open-pollinated	85 days to maturity

Comments

Delicious, productive, dependable, cold-tolerant, dark purple, Russian heirloom.

Brandywine

Indeterminate	Open-pollinated	80 days to maturity

Comments

Huge heirloom; quite possibly the *best-tasting* tomato. The original Brandywine is pink; there are also red and yellow types. Brandy Boy is a hybrid that produces larger numbers of similar fruit.

© tomatofest.com

© tomatofest.com

Photo by David Cavagnaro.

Celebrity

Determinate	Hybrid	70 days to maturity

Comments

Medium-large fruit; often flawless appearance; very disease resistant; dependable and tasty. *Observed* to be resistant to specific diseases and/or pests.

Cherokee Purple

Indeterminate	Open-pollinated	80 days to maturity

Comments

Purple-pink, delicious, super-productive heirloom; a farmer's market favorite.

Photo by David Cavagnaro.

Early Girl

Indeterminate	Hybrid	52 days to maturity

Comments

Super-dependable, *early*, productive, tasty, medium-size slicer; a classic! *Observed* to be resistant to specific diseases and/or pests.

© tomatofest.com

Georgia Streak

Indeterminate	Open-pollinated	90 days to maturity

Comments

The prettiest tomato I ever grew; huge yellow fruit with red streaks throughout and the perfect balance of sugar and acidity; very flavorful!

© tomatofest.com

German Johnson

Indeterminate	Open-pollinated	76 days to maturity

Comments

A classic pinkish-red heirloom; more productive and faster to produce than most. *Proven* to be resistant to specific diseases and/or pests.

Photo by David Cavagnaro.

Lemon Boy

Indeterminate	Open-pollinated	75 days to maturity

Comments

Light yellow color; tasty, meaty fruit; a heavy producer.

© tomatofest.com

Mortgage Lifter

Indeterminate	Open-pollinated	79 days to maturity

Comments

Biggest fruit of any tomato I've grown; delicious, pinkish-red two- to three-pounders (1kg). Radiator Charlie's Mortgage Lifter is the classic of this type.

© tomatofest.com

Oregon Spring

Determinate	Open-pollinated	60 days to maturity

Comments

Very productive and extremely cold-tolerant; a must-have for short-season growers! *Observed* to be resistant to specific diseases and/or pests.

Photo by David Cavagnaro.

Park's Whopper Improved

Indeterminate	Hybrid	65 days to maturity

Comments

An improved "crack-free" version of the classic Whopper (released in 1992 as OG 50); big tasty tomatoes that ripen very early for their size. *Observed* to be resistant to specific diseases and/or pests.

© tomatofest.com

Rutgers

Determinate	Open-pollinated	75 days to maturity

Comments

A true classic all-around tomato; pretty, productive, and very juicy. (And Rutgers just might be the "Jersey Tomato" of legend.) *Observed* to be resistant to specific diseases and/or pests.

Stupice

Indeterminate	Open-pollinated	60 days to maturity

Comments

Remarkable heirloom; *very* flavorful and *extremely* cold tolerant; productive too. Essential for short-season growing. *Observed* to be resistant to specific diseases and/or pests.

Photo by David Cavagnaro.

Tigerella (a.k.a. Mr. Stripey)

Indeterminate	Open-pollinated	60 days to maturity

Comments

An adorable little red tomato with yellow-orange stripes; tangy, productive, and early.

Amish Paste

Indeterminate	Open-pollinated	82 days to maturity

Comments

Huge semi-oxheart-shaped fruits; tasty, productive, flavorful heirloom; great all-purpose tomato.

© tomatofest.com

Opalka

Indeterminate	Open-pollinated	75 days to maturity

Comments

Large, sweet, banana-shaped fruit; very meaty Polish heirloom.

Roma

Determinate	Open-pollinated	75 days to maturity

Comments

Great taste; extraordinarily productive and dependable; *the* classic paste tomato. *Observed* to be resistant to specific diseases and/or pests.

Photo by David Cavagnaro.

San Marzano

Indeterminate	Open-pollinated	80 days to maturity

Comments
Drop-dead gorgeous fruit; *very* tasty; super-reliable; great fresh and for sauce.

CHERRIES

Green Grape

Determinate	Open-pollinated	75 days to maturity

Comments
Stays green when ripe, but tastes like a red tomato; a fun grow! Amaze your friends!

Riesentraube

Indeterminate	Open-pollinated	76 days to maturity

Comments
Translation: "Giant bunch of grapes;" flavorful heirloom; grows in clusters.

© tomatofest.com

Sun Gold

Indeterminate	Hybrid	57 days to maturity

Comments

Early yellow-orange sweetie; unique mild tropical citrusy flavor.

Supersweet 100

Indeterminate	Hybrid	63 days to maturity

Comments

Just as flavorful as the original Sweet 100, with improved disease resistance; early.

Sweet Million

Indeterminate	Hybrid	65 days to maturity

Comments

Inflationary improvement on the classic Sweet 100; early and hugely productive with larger fruit. *Observed* to be resistant to specific diseases and/or pests.

Photo by David Cavagnaro.

Photo by David Cavagnaro.

Sweet 100

| Indeterminate | Hybrid | 65 days to maturity |

Comments

The original "never-ending vine" extra-sweet cherry; *the* standard; warning: garden space hog!

Yellow Pear

| Indeterminate | Open-pollinated | 80 days to maturity |

Comments

Golden-colored, pear-shaped, super sweet–flavored heirloom; hugely productive.

I'd like to offer my thanks to my friends at Gurney's Seed & Nursery Company (*Gurneys.com*), TomatoFest® Heirloom Tomato Seeds (*www.tomatofest.com*), and David Cavagnaro for providing the photos for the chart.

Chapter 2

The Joy of Germination

(Or, Killing Your Own Tomatoes from Seed)

Now that you've selected the tomato varieties you intend to grow over the next several months, it's time to turn some tiny little seeds into gigantic plants bursting with luscious ripe fruit.

Starting tomatoes isn't *really* difficult, like growing eggplant or watermelons, but it isn't easy like growing zucchini either. Although seed starting *is* a very different endeavor than actual gardening, it really just requires that you don't screw up the important things. Think of it as a corollary to life itself—or your driving test. And yes, that means you might *not* get it right the first time.

Actually, if you are a *total* rookie gardener, you have complete permission to buy your plants already started the first year and practice killing nice big grown plants before you move on to little bitty ones.

Anyway, first, do the math. To figure out when to start your seeds, you need to have some idea of when you hope to put actual living plants out into the garden. Put those plants out too early, and the poor little babies will freeze to death. Do it too late, and you won't get as many tomatoes as you could have, unless you live in Syracuse, and then you won't get any.

So, find out what the average last frost date is for your area. Call your local Cooperative Extension office (type "Cooperative Extension" and the name of your state into an Internet search engine and it should lead you to a list of your state's local offices) and ask them what your average last frost date is. They *live* for this kind of stuff. Or just type "average last frost date" into the same search engine, and I'm sure you'll be interactively informed.

Pineapple

Pineapple is a very large, classic bicolor (yellow streaked with red) heirloom tomato type that can be found under a dozen different names. Pineapple is one of the largest—and the cleanest. At least in my garden it resists cracking and splitting, even in wet seasons, and ripens up smoother and more perfectly formed than most of my other bicolors. It's a nice love apple to show off—or maybe even enter at the county fair.

The term "Average Frost Date" has killed more tomatoes than summer hailstorms. When you get to your "AFD," check the 10-day forecast. If any nights are predicted to drop below 50 degrees Fahrenheit, do not plant. Look at this forlorn frozen thing; even if it survives (and it won't), it will be weak and sullen the rest of the season. Daytime temps don't matter—it's the nighttime lows (and Mother's Day snows) that will getcha.

Now, some books would provide a big ol' hairy chart here that reveals last frost dates for the entire nation. But the truth is that even the finest, most excellently configured of such charts usually looks like somebody used the book to swat a fly and caught it right about where your state or region should be.

But, for many of us, the date we use is simply the *average* average: If you live above the Carolinas, but not so far north that your snow shovel is still handy in June, you can typically put your plants out safely between May 15 (warmer climes) and June 1 (cool climes) and pretty much count on success. If you live in an area where it *never* frosts, well, it doesn't really much matter when you put *yours* out, now does it? *Your* plants aren't going to *freeze*, are they?

Anyway, you want to allow your seeds a week or so (call it ten days to be safe) to germinate, and a *full six weeks (they're still going to look pretty puny at that age, so no cheating!)* to grow big and strong before you consider putting them out into the cold, cruel world—which you should do only "after all chance of frost is gone."

You know what that last part means, don't you? Right—*you* will now have the power to cause the latest frost in the history of your region! It's easy! Just call up your local TV weather guesser and say, "I'm going to make it freeze on Thursday!"

"How are you going to do *that*? It's predicted to be mild—fifties at night and sixties during the day."

"I'm putting my tomatoes out on Wednesday."

"Wait a minute—hold on…Sorry—what did you say? I got distracted by the radar; looks like there's a huge cold front heading down out of Canada."

Now, where I live in Pennsylvania, the average last frost date *is* May 15. But many people have been confused into thinking this means it won't ever frost on May 16 here. Uh-uh. "*On average*" it won't. And you can imagine how much your poor plants will care about odds and averages when they're looking for scrap wood to burn in little barrels as they rapidly lose the feeling in their tiny branches, and stuff that looks suspiciously like snow begins to mulch them.

So my advice for you is to plan to put your sweet, trusting little plants in the garden about two weeks *after* your average last frost date. Freezing isn't the only factor here; tomatoes are tropical plants that have no sense of humor about temperatures in the forties, much less thirties; and unless you go to lots of trouble to keep them warm and protected, they'll just sit out there sulking until the nights are reliably in the fifties. Rush the season and you'll be starting with weakened—and possibly psychotically resentful—plants.

TIMING YOUR TOMATOES

OK, now let's say you're like me and you plan to plant on June 1, a date that has always served me well. Here's the math:

```
10 days for germination ··················· 10
6 weeks to grow    ······················· +45 (my weeks are longer than yours)
1 week to harden-off ····················· +10 (Rounded up to be safe and easy to add.
                                                And yes, we'll explain what "hardening-off" means later.)
Total ··································· = 65 days
```

So round off all the extras I added, and let's call it two months. That means you could safely start your seeds anywhere between mid-March and April 1.

Why as early as mid-March?

It won't hurt a bit if the plants are a little older (and *bigger*) when they go out, and they can certainly go out on May 15 if the ten-day forecast shows nights staying reliably in the fifties. And, what if you screw up and your first run of starts all die? Honor dictates you try again at least once before you go out and buy the strange-looking overfed Big Boys at Wal-Mart! Besides, there are a *lot* of seeds in those packets.

But you *won't* fail, and they *won't* die!

Tomato-Starting Stuff

One of the great things about seed starting is that you can go out and buy lots of stuff and actually claim you're going to save money by doing so. It's probably going to turn out to be a damned lie, but hey—the shopping is still fun. Here's what you need to get your tomato babies growing:

- ☑ Tomato seeds (duh!)
- ☑ The plastic six-packs that last year's tomato (or pepper or marigold or petunia or…) plants came in. (Don't have any among your "I may be able to use this someday" stuff? You can almost certainly get as many as you need from any long-time gardener—I've got *hundreds*!) Don't use folklore equipment like old yogurt cups or egg cartons. You need something made of plastic that drains well and is about the depth of, well, of nursery plant six-packs! Oh, and don't use peat pots or peat pellets or similar things; peat wicks moisture into the air and makes it nearly impossible to keep the plants evenly watered.

These are four-packs, which are just as good as six-packs. But there are *way* too many freaking tomatoes in these things! You're sowing tomato seed, not a lawn. Take this as an example *not* to follow.

Always use a light, loose seed-starting mix (bottom) to start your seedlings, *not* garden soil! Top off with some nice worm poop—uh, I mean "castings" (top)—when your seedlings are three to four weeks old to feed them naturally.

Do you have everything on that Tomato-Starting Stuff Checklist assembled? Good. Now, mix all the ingredients together, cover with aluminum foil, and bake in a preheated 350°F (177°C) oven for forty minutes, then...

Oh, no, wait a minute—that's the recipe for tonight's chicken casserole. Never mind.

☑ Seed-starting mix. *Not* your lousy garden soil! No, no, no. Listen to me now and this becomes the first time I save the life of your tomatoes-to-be. Your tender charges *will* be dead if you ignore this warning! You want soil-free mix, and *not* one of the soil-free mixes that has chemical fertilizers added. You may have to shop around a bit to find a clean bag of the right stuff, but it is *essential*. More on this in a bit.

☑ Something to sit the six-packs in that will hold them and water, like an old baking dish or one of those big aluminum trays that the caterer left behind (check for pinholes in the bottom first!), or even—call me crazy—one of those plastic flats (the sans-hole kind) that actual plant professionals use for holding plastic six-packs of seedlings.

☑ A fluorescent shop light with two or four 40-watt tubes that are each four feet (1200 millimeters) long. No, your sunny windowsill is *not* good enough. ("Sunny windowsill" is actually Latin for "that's why your plants died.") And two foot (600 millimeter)-long tubes or 25-watt ones aren't good enough either. On the other hand, a *four*-tube fixture *is* way better than a deuce.

☑ Something to eventually feed the young plants with, like a little finished compost, some worm castings (excellent fertilizer and no smell), or a nice gentle organic fertilizer, like a liquid seaweed/fish mixture. (Note: Fish fertilizers *do* have a smell, so you probably want to reserve them for outside use.)

Ready, Set, Start!

About that seed-starting mixture: One of the secrets of your impending success will be the fact that you wisely chose *not* to use your lousy garden soil (LGS) to start your seeds. That's because your LGS will turn into concrete and kill the poor things even faster than you can imagine. I don't care how great you think your dirt is, your little sprouties need a nice loose mix that both retains moisture *and* drains well. Impossible, you say? Nay, say I!

Anyway, once you've been doing this for a few years, the ideal way to achieve this mixture is to make it yourself. You buy a bag of perlite, which looks like little Styrofoam balls, but is actually an incredibly lightweight, mined, "popped" mineral; a bag of vermiculite, which looks like little pieces off the back of a broken mirror but is also lightweight, natural, mined stuff; and a bale of milled peat moss—which is, well, it's peat moss. Moisten the materials to cut down on dust, and mix them together in a big galvanized tub or wheelbarrow. *Do this outdoors and wear a dust mask; you don't want to breathe a lot of any kind of dust.*

Add a very small amount of hardwood ash from a woodstove or fireplace (or lime) to balance the acidity of the peat moss—say a tablespoon or so of ash or lime per quart (liter) of peat. Then mix in some nice, finished, high-quality black compost—up to about one quarter of the total. If you don't have your own compost, you can buy it in a bag if you absolutely *have* to, but first try to bum some from a gardening friend. Homemade compost is the *best* compost! (And if you really can't find *any*, mix in some worm castings instead.)

So that's:

      1 part perlite
      1 part vermiculite
      1 part peat moss
      1 part compost
      Teeny tiny bit of lime or wood ash

But the *first* year you start your own seeds, you should instead invest your energy in finding a nice pre-mixed bag of seed-starting (aka "soil-free") mix to which you will add some compost. Buy this bag by weight, but in reverse: If the bag feels at all heavy for its size, take a pass! If the bag seems impossibly light for its size, you've got the right stuff. But be sure to check the label to see what's in that fluffy light bag. Some mix makers think they're doing you a favor by tossing chemical fertilizer ("feeds plants for three months; makes your garden non-organic for three years!") or water-holding crystals into the mix. But just say no. Your little plants don't need none of that extra stuff around their roots.

You can make your own seed-starting mixture with ingredients such as perlite (top), peat moss (middle), and vermiculite (bottom). Add some wood ash or lime to counteract the acidity of the peat moss.

Note: Mixes labeled "potting soil" may be the right stuff (the weight of the bag will tell the tale), but "potting soil" can also be a synonym for lead and bricks mixed together in a bag.

An open-pollinated super-sweet heirloom paste tomato, **Yellow Pear** is praised for its high sugar content. Make a dedicated batch of sauce from this variety alone and label it "Liquid Gold!"

The Main Event!

OK, now comes the fun part! Fill your containers with the seed-starting mix, leaving an inch (25 millimeters) or so of space at the top of the containers. But don't plant any seeds yet. First, put the containers into their dishes, pour water into the dishes, and go watch TV or something for an hour while the mix absorbs the water. If the dish is dry when you come back, add a little water, and keep doing this until water starts to pool up in the bottom of the dish, despite time having passed. Then, place *two seeds* in each six-pack cell. If you're starting more than one variety, keep a chart of which variety is where. *Don't use Popsicle sticks or other big plant markers yet.* I put colored twist ties into the dirt of each six-pack and then write down which variety name goes with each twist tie color. Figure out a method that works for you; just be sure to mark your plants somehow so you won't get confused when you move the six-packs around.

Then cover the seeds with a little more of the mix, somewhere around a quarter to half an inch (5 to 15 millimeters). You can now mist the top of your freshly planted seed bed with a gentle sprayer (Your mister *must* be clean—don't use a sprayer that previously had chemicals, vinegar, or anything other than water in it!), or just add a little more water to the bottom of the dish. *Don't* water from above with anything stronger than a mist—your seeds will wash into each other's parking spots, you won't know what's where, and you'll be confused and discouraged, and you haven't even gotten anything really started yet.

Now, cover the top of the whole shebang with a loose sheet of plastic wrap (don't make it tight and clingy) to help keep things moist. Then, place this extremely professional setup someplace where it stays nice and warm—70° to 75°F (21° to 24°C) is ideal. If you want guaranteed success, invest in one of those little seed-starting heating mats; it'll keep the temperature perfect for your tomatoes-to-be. Otherwise, generally the two best places in the average home are:

1) on top of the refrigerator, where the warm air from the compressor wafts up; or

2) on top of the TV set, where a gentle warm air also tends to rise. *Warning:* Avoid this second option if you're in the habit of throwing things at your Idiot Box, or if your TV isn't as flat-topped and stable as mine (otherwise your wet soil and seeds might slide down the back of your TV right in the middle of your favorite "Hogan's Heroes" episode).

If you have no such place in your layout (or one that's agreeable to your spouse; seed-starting time can bring out the marriage counselors faster than a Midlife Crisis Car suddenly appearing in the driveway), just leave them out on a counter in an evenly heated room, away from radiators, drafts (especially from doors that go outside), red Kryptonite, evil spirits, and energetic dogs whose whip-like tails leave a mark the size of a baseball bat.

Examine your precious babies every day. Lift off the plastic to let them breathe a bit and check the moisture level of their dirt.

If the top of the soil is obviously moist and no sprouts are visible, don't do anything. Put the plastic back on top and put them back in their warm spot.

If the surface seems dry, give it a spritzing or add a little water to the bottom of the holding tray. Don't go nuts; there shouldn't be water *sitting* in the bottom of that dish—*ever*. We're going for the delicate balance of always moist, but never sopping wet. Hey, if it was *easily* attainable it wouldn't be a goal, now would it?

In maybe five days, but certainly after a week, you should see the first sprouts push up out of the soil. Take the plastic off as soon as you see the *first* little green one pokin' up. Don't wait for all the sprouts to appear; remove the plastic at the sight of the very first one—and discontinue any bottom heat at this point.

BIG SEED-STARTING NO-NOS

Do *not* place your precious seedlings-to-be:

- On top of a radiator or near any other source of extreme heat. Two words: baked dirt.

- On a "sunny windowsill." Put a thermometer there. I bet it cranks up to 90°F (32°C) when the sun blazes in during the day and drops to a toasty 42°F (6°C) in the middle of the night. That's an interrogation chamber, not a seed-starting location.

LIGHT THE LIGHTS!

This is where most people fall down. Hard. Your young sprouts now need *light!* Good strong light to make them grow up thick and strong and stocky like the garden center ones, not like seven-foot-five-inch tall basketball players who weigh 140 pounds. Provide too little light and that's what you *will* get—tall, spindly plants that are desperately trying to reach above the trees they feel they must be surrounded by.

And your so-called sunny windowsill hasn't gotten any less fatal in the past week or so.

Now, if you have the *perfect* windowsill—windows and walls so well-insulated that it *never* gets too cold at night, *and* you can gauge the exact perfect distance to place the plants away from the window so they don't get fried when the sun comes blasting in but still get enough light to grow up stocky, *and* you keep that window clean (on *both* sides), *and* you turn the plants a quarter turn at least once every day…they might not look *too* pitiful after six weeks.

> After a week or so, you should see sprouts pushing up out of the soil. Yes, this will really happen. And yes, you will feel really good about it.

These baby tomatoes will grow up tall and skinny on this "sunny windowsill"; good for basketball players and Major League pitchers, but not for tomatoes. Spring for the artificial light, cheapskate!

IMPORTANT LIGHTING UPDATE FOR THE NEW EDITION

When the very first edition of this book was published (the dinosaurs were gone, but giant cave bears still roamed the earth), four-foot-long (1.2-meter-long) fluorescent tubes were fat (sorry—they were "short for their weight"). Modern fluorescents—currently called "T8"s—are skinny, more energy efficient, and contain little to no mercury. Old-school tubes had a fair amount of "the only metal that is liquid at room temperature." (A fact I learned from the old 1960s DC comic "The Metal Men" [whose ranks included a really hot female Metal Person named Platinum on whom I had a crush long after you should have a crush on paper or Platinum. She was *really* cute. Really.].)

If you have an old-school setup, I would urge you to move up to T8s; it's the right thing to do, they're not expensive, and you should use new bulbs (of any fluorescent type) for seed-starting every season. (The old bulbs are fine for lighting a room but will have lost a lot of the lumens young starts need.)

What did he just say? **"LUMENS"?** Is that a band?

Close. Search the Lumineers.

Simply put (which is how I simply put things), lumens are a measure of light intensity, like candle power (note: do *not* start your seeds by candlelight—that's why they called them the Dark Ages). The more lumens, the brighter the light. The brighter the light, the stockier your starts will be. When you shop for bulbs, look for information on the paper sleeve and/or one end of the naked bulb. The average for four-footers (1.2-meter-longs) is said to be about 2850 lumens, but I looked around and found 3200 and 3400 ones.

A note about watts. Hell of a guitarist, isn't he? Oh—electrical usage, not Charlie.

Anywhose, wattage (like the classic 40-watt fluorescents I used to use) is only related to power draw, not brightness. Those of us who are a certain age (I remember calling TI6-1212 to have The Time Lady help me set my watch) were conditioned to know that an old-school incandescent rated at 100 watts was almost twice as bright as a 60 watt (and five times brighter than my brother). But that equation is no longer true for modern lighting. My old-school 40-watt four-foot (1.2-meter) tubes only consume 32 watts of power in their newer T8 incarnation.

And now a woid about LEDs. New on the scene, light-emitting diodes are the latest bee's knees. Unlike fluorescents, there's no possibility of mercury or other bad actors in the mix, you don't have to swap them out every year, they literally cost pennies to run (how will we pay for them if they stop making pennies?!), and their light is directional. That means all the light shines down on your plants; fluorescents shine all around, including behind the tubes, where you (hopefully) don't have any plants. Yes, LEDs are more expensive. But if I were a young man just starting out (*deep* sigh), I would start out with LEDs. Just make sure the lumens are rated somewhere around 3000.

Come on—the shop light costs $10 when it's *not* on sale, and the 40-watt tubes'll cost you a couple bucks more. And when your tomatoes go out to the garden, you can put houseplants like African violets under the light and make them happier than they've ever been. Or you could take it down to light your shop.

Anyway, rig the light up with the chains that will doubtless accompany it so you can raise the fixture up as the plants grow. Or, start out with your setup resting on bricks or books or something else you can remove as the need arises, because you need to keep the tops of your precious plants *really* close to those life-giving bulbs.

Position your tender sprouts so there's about an inch (25 millimeters) between them and the lights. That's a *real* inch, by the way, not a foot or six inches or two-and-a-half—you want these babies *close*. And as they grow taller and stronger, you want to maintain that one-inch (25-millimeter) distance from the lights. That's why we use fluorescents—the light they produce is cool; the bulbs don't get hot and so don't harm the plants. Which is good, because the plant-useful light intensity of fluorescent bulbs drops off sharply after an inch (25 millimeters) or so. You *have* to keep plants and bulbs in each other's personal space to get fat, happy, young tomato starts.

You can leave these lights on twenty-four/seven or put them on a timer that gives them eight hours of darkness every evening. I personally have blown the transformer down at the end of the block doing things like trying to set a timer, so I just leave my lights on all the time. Most people will tell you to turn the lights off for eight hours or so every night to simulate darkness. But darkness is the *last* thing my tomatoes need. They're going to get plenty of that out in my shade-infested garden.

This energy-efficient glass tube is *the* secret to growing short, stocky, happy, and healthy tomato plants. If you turn it on, of course…

Very important: Do *not* cheat on the distance between plant tops and bulb lights or turn the lights off for more than eight hours a day. While these fluorescents do give off a nice shine o' light, they aren't the giant, exploding, plant-growing nuclear reactor around which we orbit, and to which your tomatoes will soon be exposed. Turn the lights off for *more* than eight hours at night (or cheat on the distance between the plants and the tubes) and you risk your plants getting "leggy" instead of "stocky"—desirable perhaps for people, but not for baby tomato plants. Your young starts will be grateful for any extra light you give them. Spindly, leggy starts are not worth planting.

And don't worry, you fellow twenty-four/seven transformer blowers out there, your "all light, all the time" plants will do just fine when they finally experience night. (Hey, up in Alaska it doesn't get dark for *months* and people there don't develop early blight as a result.)

Oh, and try not to let your growing starts get too hot or cold. Somewhere close to 70°F (21°C) during the day would be ideal. Nighttime temps can be a little lower—a ten to fifteen degree differential is actually beneficial for your plants—but don't let it drop below 55°F (10°C). Note: If you're growing your starts in a real greenhouse (show off!), make sure it vents automatically during sunny days and closes up when the temperature inside drops down to 60°F (16°C) or so. You don't need artificial light in a greenhouse, but you *do* need automatic temperature control.

The next month and a half will be the easiest in this adventure. The most important thing you have to do now is *not overwater*!

Got that? Good. Now find a place where you can shimmy a toothpick down an inch (25 millimeters) or so into your soil and check thusly every other day or so. If it's dry a couple of inches down, *then* you can water—still from the bottom.

The best method is to take your start-containing dishes out to the sink, put an inch (25 millimeters) or so of cool clean water in them, wait a half hour, pour out any water in the bottom of the dish, and return your well-soaked sprouts to their under-the-light positions. Depending

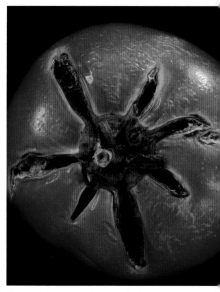

Overwatering can ruin your plants at any stage in their life, from the very beginnings through to when your tomatoes are ripening—and cracking!

on your indoor humidity, you may need to do this every day, every other day, or only once a week. So *don't* try to go by a schedule, go by the tale of the toothpick. As you gain experience, you'll be able to determine your sprouts' water needs by the weight of their six-packs. Containers full of plants that need water are almost impossibly light; saturated six-packs are very heavy.

Get a little pair of scissors and clip off the plant with the skinnier stalk to give the stockier seedling more room.

SPEAKING OF BEING BRAVE...

When your plants have what are called their first true leaves (the tomato plant–shaped ones, not the little round ones that pop up first to check out the neighborhood) it's thinning time!

You put two seeds into each cell because there's always the occasional bad seed that doesn't want to sprout. But you don't want to keep both of the plants you'll now have in most of those little cells. Nope. Their *wittle woots* need *woom* to *gwow*, and "doubles" planted outside often yield *no* tomatoes. So only one plant in each little container is bound for your garden; its slender cellmate must give its life for the greater good of the garden.

Yes, you *have* to do this. And no, you can't just *pull* out the weaker one—you must carefully *snip* it off at the soil line. The roots of the two plants are already all wrapped up together, and if you yank, you'll pull the whole shebang out. Snip off the tallest, skinniest or otherwise weakest-looking one (or ones if you had a heavy hand with the seeding). Keep the shortest, stockiest, most nicely colored sibling.

After you've removed the doubles, give the survivors their first feeding. Instead of just water, give them a nice drink of compost tea (see "Compost Tea" on page 79) or a very dilute (half the strength it says on the label) solution of a nice balanced organic fertilizer, like a seaweed concoction or a fish and seaweed mix (warning: odoriferous when used inside). This will now replace every other watering—that is, from here on out when your babies need moisture, you should alternate between plain old water and dilute liquid fertilizer. Pour off any extra fertilizing liquid into your houseplants (unless it's fishy) or on the ground around your roses outside or something. Alternative: carefully place half an inch (15 millimeters) of worm castings (widely available and a *great* plant food) on the surface of the soil every one to two weeks.

Potting up. Depending on the size of your original six-packs, you may want/need to move your starts into larger containers when they're a month or so old. This is actually pretty close to easy-peasy. The new container should be half again as large, and have the same great drainage as the original. (I use the *individual* plastic pots that nurseries sell herbs and larger started plants in.) Spread out a bunch of newspapers to keep the counter clean, take your six-packs, and squeeze the sides of the cells gently. Soil and plants should come out in one piece. Place these "plugs" into the *bottom* of the new container and add soil-free mix and/or compost and/or worm castings to fill in the sides and top. Because of a unique trait we'll soon discuss, the plants should always go into the very *bottom* of the new container whenever you repot. (Note: This is *not* true for other plants, just tomatoes.) If your package crumbles on exiting its cell, don't worry—just get the root hairs down as low as you can in the new container while still leaving an inch or two (25 to 50 millimeters) of plant showing above the soil line when you're finished.

COUNTDOWN TO GREATNESS!

If you've gotten this far and have a nice-looking crop of young plants, you're over the hump, baby! Keep them under those lights, water sparingly, and start planning your outdoor placement—because as soon as they're old enough (six to eight weeks) and it stays warm enough (nighttime temps that are mostly in the fifties; some high forties are OK [about 7° to 10°C], but nothing colder—you'll just be rushing the poor babies), we're going outside!

Eventually your seedlings should be repotted into larger temporary homes to avoid becoming "pot bound"—like that annoying teenager next door. This is one happy love apple!

News flash:
Do *not* water every day unless your six-packs are light in weight and their soil is bone dry every day! Your plants will rot and drown and die! (And if you do *need* to water every day, get a humidifier.) All plants need to dry out between waterings. Better to underdo it a little than overdo it on this one.

Chapter 3

The Art of Tomato Planting

· ·

(You want me to *bury* them?)

By now you should have either nice, stocky six- to eight-week-old tomato plants you started yourself from seed, or plants of unknown origin you bought at a garden center because you were too chicken to try what I told you last chapter.

If you don't have your own tomato plants ready to go, and the time is right for planting, stop reading *right now* and go out and purchase some nice stocky starts. "Stocky" sounds so much nicer than "short and fat," but that's what it means and that is indeed what you want—at least in tomato plants.

Hardening Off

This is actually very important—especially if you started your own plants from seed. What we want to do here is get those puppies gradually acclimated to the conditions outdoors, which are colder, possibly wetter, possibly drier, and almost certainly more treacherous in every way possible than the wonderfully controlled indoor weather you've been providing. And no—you *can't* just keep them indoors with you. They're tomatoes, not cats.

> By now you should have either nice, stocky six- to eight-week-old tomato plants you started yourself from seed or plants of unknown origin you bought at a garden center because you didn't do what I told you to last chapter. (If that's the case, don't worry—it's all right; we don't judge. Well, OK—maybe we *do* judge. But you'll start with seed next year, right? Don't make me write another edition just for you.)

Viva Italia

Viva Italia is a classic Italian paste tomato variety. Paste (or plum) tomatoes are bred to contain more meat (solids) and less liquid than standard (fresh eating) varieties, which really helps speed up the cooking of sauce and paste. And many people prefer the reduced mess on sandwiches compared to bigger, more juicy tomatoes.

Give your plants a chance to acclimate to the harsh real world.

Take your tomato plants outside and let them enjoy the outdoors for an hour or two. Then bring them back in and say, "Nice tomato plants! Good tomato plants!"

Once it gets close to your region's ideal outdoor tomato-planting time, keep an eye on the weather and look for a stretch where mild temperatures are expected to prevail for several days in a row and not be immediately followed by a raging blizzard. If it's going to stay really nasty out for a while, don't worry about what the calendar says or how many weeks old your plants are. Better to let them get a little overgrown indoors than freeze to death, drown, or otherwise join the Choir Invisible.

Putting them out into nasty cold weather because you're afraid it's getting too late in the season has *nothing* going for it. Unprotected tomatoes will just sit there (if you're lucky and they don't kick the bucket outright) and refuse to grow until temps warm up. Same goes for folks who jumped the season with purchased plants; *don't* put them out into wretchedness. Give them the best indoor light you can, don't feed or overwater them, and maybe make a ritual sacrifice to The Weather Channel to try and move things along.

OK—let's say we've got a nice day coming up with a prediction of decent weather the week after. Put your tomato plants outside for an hour or two during the day. Then bring them back in. The next day, leave them out a little longer; same for the next day. Depending on the weather and your tolerance for this kind of thing, you will soon leave them out overnight. This should *not* be a night when it is expected to be really chilly, rainy, or the like. And *snow* is totally out.

Yes, this seems tedious, but this specific act of tediousness provides bigger rewards than most of the other ones. And be warned: if you ignore this advice and just plant the suckers right there in the ground straight from the house, your pretty little tomato plants may well lie down and take long nappies. Perhaps forever, depending on just how poor the weather and your judgment are.

Tomatoes that are *not* hardened off go into shock. It's kind of like when you were born—you left that warm little liquid bubble where you had floated blissfully for *so* long and where nothing bothered you and then—*boom!* You're surrounded by bright lights, loud noises, and a guy in a mask slapping your keister. No wonder you cried.

Don't do this to your tomatoes.

By letting your plants get used to the outdoors gradually, you'll prevent them from experiencing transplant shock. And your reward will be bigger, happier, healthier plants that will grow faster, produce more tasty tomatoes, and be better able to naturally resist disease and pest attacks all summer long.

And they won't die right away, either. That's always a plus.

Location, Location, Location

Tomatoes really are among the easiest plants you can grow—that's one reason why so many folks grow 'em. (All of the other reasons are related to the grower's ethnic background and/or the non-flavor of supermarket tomatoes.) You should be aware that tomatoes are originally native to a region (Peru) where their leaves almost never get wet. When we grow them in other places, rain and general dampness make them prone to certain diseases. You can *greatly limit*—perhaps even prevent—such problems by choosing a spot to grow your love apples that is not conducive to disease.

You'll always get more and better quality tomatoes from raised beds than flat earth. Now will somebody please fill these ones up?!

Actually make that more than one spot. In a kitchen garden, you should always try to avoid grouping all your plants of *any* one kind in one spot. If, for instance, you have eight tomato plants and eight raised beds, I suggest you place one plant in each bed instead of filling up, say, two of the beds with all your tomato plants.

Many of your finer tomatoes—including all of your heirlooms and big beefsteak sandwich types—grow on big honking plants that no one ever allows enough room for. Many is the time I've pulled up a frost-killed fourteen-foot-or-longer Brandywine or Mortgage Lifter vine at the end of the season and discovered that, "oh, *that's* where that missing hot pepper, cucumber, and/or eggplant was!" *And* the tomato plant had been "restrained" inside a cage.

Plant a whole bunch of tomatoes in one bed and you risk crowding your plants together so much they will soon become one giant tangled heap of vines that can't dry out and are just begging for disease to come calling. So plant them apart *and* plant them apart. Don't group them all together, *and* do leave plenty of room between your tomatoes—and other large plants as well. You can plant herbs and little flowers around them; it won't hurt, and it'll look pretty. And yes, this is/that was our Martha Stewart Moment.

Grouping all of your plants of the same type together really lends a helping hand to pests and diseases. Once a bad bug or plant sickness finds one of your tomatoes, it will notice that other such plants are handily adjacent, enabling it to spread its negative effects faster than a bad winter cold in a day care center. Numerous research studies have found that simply mixing up your plantings greatly limits the spread of disease and confuses and discourages garden pests.

Wouldn't it have been nice if, before you were thrust into the cold, cruel world, your mom had given you a little peek at the outside, at your older brothers and sisters who were gearing up to spend the rest of their lives tormenting you, and at all the other nice things that awaited your entrance, and then popped you back in for a while and eased you out gradually over the course of a week or so? Well, you can do for your tomatoes what your mom couldn't do for you!

Don't forget to take them out of their pots!

WE'RE ALMOST THERE

If you plan your garden this way, take notes when you plant so you can remember in subsequent seasons *where* in each bed you previously planted your tomatoes. Maybe make it easy and plant your tomatoes on the left-hand side of each bed the first season. Then, next year, plant your tomatoes at the opposite end of each bed and the following year in the middle. Or carefully mark tomato locations with a circle of Popsicle sticks or something similar when you pull the plants up at the end of the season. (You know, I kind of like the idea of little Popsicle Stonehenges appearing in gardens all around the country…) But do *something*, because you *really* want to avoid planting tomatoes (and some other crops, but mostly and especially tomatoes) in the same spot season after season. If you ignore this advice, soil-borne diseases like *verticillium* and *fusarium wilt will* take hold and attack your plants. How long do you have to wait until a spot is tomato safe again? Nobody knows for *sure*, but a three-year rotation is a good bet.

And if you're a lucky person who has lots of gardening room (I'll try not to dislike you for this, but I got a postage stamp surrounded by forest), you can *position* your plants perfectly as well. "Perfect" is where they will get the first possible rays of the morning sun. Morning sun burns off nighttime dampness quickly, and a dry tomato plant is a happy tomato plant. Conversely, if your tomato plants have to wait until the afternoon to enjoy the drying rays of the sun, they'll be miserable, prone to disease, and may report you to the police. Corn and cabbages couldn't care less about morning sun. *Hostas* don't need *any* sun. But tomato plants (and roses and lilacs) love and need morning rays.

Now, before we digs our hole, we wants to makes sure:

- the plants won't be crowded when they reach full size (which is roughly 6,000 times bigger than they are now, give or take a hundredfold or so);

- they aren't all grouped together unless you deliberately want to plant them all in one or two *big, humongously large* beds with enough room for a foot (300 millimeters) of open space between each *fully grown* plant so you can rotate them to different beds next year, *ensuring* that you won't follow tomatoes with tomatoes. This can actually be a very good strategy—but only if you give each plant lots of room; and

- they're in a spot in the garden that gets the most and earliest morning sun and are out in the open with good air circulation all around (don't plant them up against a wall or where they'll be surrounded by other tall plants).

Yes, I do realize that in the real world, few people can achieve *all* of these things. But what I have described is the ideal situation, and the closer you get to it, the happier we'll all be. For instance: Can't manage morning sun? Then make *sure* the plants are out in the open, with good air circulation all around. Crowding is more of an irreparable issue, however. If you're Seriously Short on Space, you may have to give away a few of your plants, grow your extras in a nearby community garden (or the temporarily seized land of an understanding friend; they get half the haul), or in containers, because crowding *will* hurt you. You'll get a lot more fruit from two plants with elbow room than you will from six plants crammed into the equivalent of an un-air-conditioned subway car at rush hour.

OK. Now, think about the areas you have available that meet those requirements—or at least some of them. But also relax; the odds are good that you'll do fine and have fun, even if you have to bend the rules a little.

This is not a test. In fact, figuring out where to plant your tomatoes is generally not an educational experience of *any* kind (especially in my garden). Nor can it be reasonably expected to be an *uplifting* experience. No, tomato growing is more like opera. Forget wish fulfillment; this is an *artistic* experience, and you *will* enjoy what you get out of it.

Unless all your plants die, of course.

Anyway, now that we've got the site picked out, we're *finally* ready to plant. OK—*almost* finally ready. Hey, don't worry—things get moving pretty quickly after this.

Always remove the leaves from the lower half of the plant and plant it deeper than you think you should.

Growing tomatoes is like painting a house: preparation is everything. You paint a room, and it takes you two weeks to scrape, peel, clean, spackle, sand, apply painter's tape, and otherwise prepare the surface and about twenty minutes to actually fling on the paint. And remember what the wall looked like that time you didn't scrape, spackle, peel, and clean, and you ran out of painter's tape and used Scotch tape instead? You don't want to see that again, do you?

Raised beds are a great option for growing tomatoes. They give your plants enough room to grow (if you remember not to put eight plants in one bed), keep you from trampling all over their soil, and can help you keep track of which variety of tomato plant you put where.

Photo by Fox Chapel Publishing.

Making Your Soil Slightly Less Lousy

If your soil is already compost-enriched and nice and loose, you may skip down to "Burying Your Plants with Garbage" on page 57. If, however, you are among the *other* 96 percent of the population and have really lousy soil, you should improve it first. Whether lousy because of clay, lousy from years of soil compaction, or just plain lousy, a little bit of "double-digging" can do wonders for poor soil. Strenuous, but not complicated, double-digging is little more than taking a lot of dirt out of the ground and then putting it back in again. Yes, it *does* sound remarkably like Army work, but the process really loosens up the soil and allows your tomato plants' roots to breathe and reach down deep for moisture and nutrients. This is especially important if you, like me here in Pennsylvania, have a lot of heavy clay.

> You might not know this, but "Pennsylvania" is actually a Native American word that means "soil so thick you can make terra-cotta pots just by spinning your hand in the ground."

DOUBLE-DIGGING 101

First, dig a trench across the area where you want to plant, about a foot (300 millimeters) or so wide and just as deep. If you're growing in raised beds (which I would explain in detail, but if I do that, we'll *never* get these puppies in the ground), you'll want to double-dig the whole bed, of course. A bed, by the way, should never be more than four feet (1200 millimeters) wide, raised or not; you need to be able to reach everything in the bed without stepping on your nice loose soil and making it crappy again. Compacted soil is the second largest human cause of plant death—overwatering will always be number one. The lanes around such beds should always be two feet (600 millimeters) wide so you can walk around the beds without stepping in them.

Toss the soil into a wheelbarrow or onto a tarp, removing rocks and any large, obvious hunks of pure clay as you go. Then, get a digging fork (the garden kind, *not* the kitchen utensil) or some other long, strong spikey thing and jab it into the ground at the bottom of the hole repeatedly to improve the drainage.

Repeat this act of soil removing and spiking in foot-long (300-millimeter) increments for the length of the bed or row, filling in each prepared trench with the newly removed soil from the next one over. When you're done with the last row, bust up the soil in the wheelbarrow or tarp with the side of a shovel or hoe and use that to fill in the last trench. Toss all of the rocks and big chunks of clay away. Using them in the bed will not make your tomatoes happy. And don't feel bad—after twenty plus years of double-digging and literally *tons* of added compost, I still find enough clods of clay in my garden beds every season to supply a college pottery class for several semesters. If you wind up with not a lot of soil left, that's great—now you've got room to put some good stuff into that bed.

Now, if for some strange reason (like heavy physical labor having lost all of its attraction) double-digging lacks appeal for you, use a rotary tiller. A power tiller is especially useful if you have a big garden, are breaking ground for a brand new garden, can't double-dig personally, and/or leap at every excuse to operate noisy power equipment. And whether you intend to dig *or* till, make sure the soil is nice and dry all the way down before you begin—otherwise it'll clump up in unpleasantly irreversible ways and you'll kill lots of earthworms. When the soil is nice and dry, the worms aren't *at* tilling level—they're down deep where the soil is damp, complaining about the noise.

While tilling, be sure to toss as many rocks and clods of clay as possible. And be warned that your arms will continue to vibrate as if you were still tilling for the next four days.

> Contrary to popular opinion, an earthworm sliced in half during the digging process does *not* yield two happy littler worms. In fact, it rarely yields one live worm—and he's never happy about it.

GET SMART ABOUT COMPOST

Don't use compost made with treated sewage sludge (aka bio solids)—too many morons and criminals still pour industrial chemicals, motor oil, and the like down their terlets and into the sewers, ruining what otherwise would be nice stuff to grow in.

Compost in a bag is acceptable, but not nearly as good as homemade, municipal, or aged mushroom soil. Bulk compost from places with big piles of nice-looking stuff sitting outside is probably OK. Here's how to tell for sure:

- It should look like rich, black "super-soil."

- It should have no "off" or foul odors; it can smell a little sweet or earthy, but nothing that makes you turn up your nose.

- It should not contain any recognizable wood chips or other "original ingredients."

- When you pick some up in your hand and squeeze it, it should have the consistency of a damp, wrung-out sponge.

- Lots of worms living in it are a very good sign.

Note: Both tilling and double digging *will* expose lots of buried weed seeds to the germinating power of sunshine, and *you* will then carefully cover them with soil, thus planting weeds. The best solution is to create a stale seed bed. Level out the tilled soil, water it, wait ten days, and then use a sharp hoe to slice off all the new young helpless weeds at the soil line.

If you can't do that, at least be aware that *They Are Coming.* Be prepared to hoe them as they pop up and have a good mulch ready to smother the stragglers. And don't directly seed anything in such a bed; you'd never be able to figure out who's who.

In future years, *don't* till *or* double-dig. Keep your feet off the growing area (*the* biggest benefit of growing in raised beds and/or any well-defined area less than four feet [1200 millimeters] wide), and the soil will stay nice and loose. Whatever you do, don't till every year—even if you really enjoy doing it (yes, I know *exactly* who you are!); repeated tilling depletes soil nutrients.

OK—now we'll add some good stuff to your still-lousy-but-now-tilled soil.

"What will we add?"

"*Compost!*"

"When will we add it?"

"*Now!*"

Anyway, the compost you make yourself from shredded leaves, coffee grounds, and small amounts of other nonmeat kitchen garbage is the best possible amendment you can add to your soil. The only thing better is high-quality homemade compost bummed from a fellow gardener (because you didn't have to make it).

Next best is municipal compost made from collected fall leaves and other yard waste, which many municipalities provide free to their residents. If your city or township has a place to take yard waste for recycling, you can probably get free compost there because that's what they recycle the stuff into. Take home *lots* of this "black gold" for your garden. (Get some for me while you're there!)

Note: Again, do *not* use bio solids or other forms of sewage sludge from water treatment plants. Some municipalities try to pass this stuff off as compost, but it is not. It is human waste containing shockingly high amounts of prescription medication residue and potentially toxic waste that villains and idiots flushed into the sewers instead of disposing of it properly.

Aged mushroom soil (aka mushroom compost, spent mushroom soil, etc.) purchased in bulk can be really good compost, but it has to be aged (cool to the touch and with an agreeable odor), not fresh (hot and stinky). In a pinch, packaged (bagged) composts can also be very good, but look for a premium, branded product with details about its contents and origins. Don't buy the generic bag that just says "Compost." And not composted *manure* either.

Alright—if you are tilling or turning your dirt, mix lots of that fine compost into your loosened-up soil as you go.

If you've got an existing bed where the soil is already nice and loose, just layer an inch or two (25 or 50 millimeters) of fresh compost on the surface of your enviable soil. Applying your compost to the surface is *never* a bad idea; it never *needs* to be tilled in, and doing so year after year would invite endless weed woes with no weward.

Note: If you have *sandy* soil, you're in luck. Just mix an equal amount of compost and/or screened black high-quality topsoil in with your sand and you create the perfect growing medium—a soil that now holds moisture and nutrients, but that drains well during wet times.

Alright, your soil is loose and rich. Now look up to the sky like a farmer in a big-screen movie. The music swells. The clouds part. A ray of sunshine strikes the very spot you've improved so well. You're ready to plant. Life is good.

BURYING YOUR PLANTS WITH GARBAGE

OK—we be planting! Now, prepare yourself, because you are about to come very close to burying your poor charges alive. Really. Tomatoes develop auxiliary roots along any part of their stem that is buried. This is good. Those extra roots can reach *lots* more water and nutrients than the roots of an unburied plant, and they also help anchor what will hopefully become a big honkin' plant in the ground. When I plant, I bury the bottom three-quarters of my tomato starts underground; just the top four inches (100 millimeters) or so are left above the soil line.

There are two different ways to do this:

1) In really cold climates. Bury your stems "trench-style." Dig your hole, fill it halfway back up with your loosened soil mixed with compost, add your crushed-up eggshells (see "The Eggshell Thing" on page 59), lay the plant stem down horizontally on top of the soil, and *gently* bend the last four inches (100 millimeters) or so straight up. Cover the to-be-buried section with at least two inches (50 millimeters)—four inches (100 millimeters) would be ideal—of your soil mix. You are following this

Homemade compost is great, but too much kitchen waste in the mix will make things nasty. "Dry browns," like shredded fall leaves, should always be in the majority.

procedure because your cold soil takes *forever* to warm up in the spring, especially down deep. By placing the rooted section close to the surface, you keep it in the warmest possible soil while still getting the benefits of the buried stem.

2) In warm to normal climates. You should *not* trench. The warmer your region gets in the summer, the more *your* tomatoes' roots will *enjoy* wiggling around in deep, cool soil. So fill in your hole with loosened soil and compost until you can place the root ball of your plant against the bottom of the hole and have just a few inches of the top of the plant poking out into the world. Remove any leaves that would otherwise be underground, plop the plant in the hole, and fill the hole with more soil and compost and some of them eggshells, tamping it down lightly. Don't go nuts with the tamping! *No* plant likes compacted soil.

Note: To get your plants safely out of their containers (like plastic nursery six-packs), squeeze the outside of each container gently all around until the plant and its soil slide or pop out easily. Try not to disturb that big clump of soil around the roots.

There are several different grape tomato varieties out there (including Green Grape, which pretty much perfects the illusion—and allusion—of its name by staying green when ripe [it's often close to seedless as well]). All grape tomato plants, including this **Red Grape,** produce bountiful clusters of little grape-shaped tomatoes, and are highly favored by tomato snackers who like to pick quarts of the little candy-like fruit at a time.

Other note: I realize it may be inconvenient, but try hard not to plant your tomatoes (or anything else, really) in the morning or even early afternoon of a hot and sunny day. Your tomatoes will *not* like roasting in the sun for hours after you manhandle them into their now hole-of-death. If it's a cloudy day, plant anytime. Otherwise, the early evening—say from 4 to 7 p.m. (or later if you're like me and often garden with the aid of a flashlight duct-taped to a pith helmet)—is the ideal time. It allows the plants all evening, night, and morning to get acclimated before they have to take those solar rays.

THE EGGSHELL THING: MIKE MCG'S SUPER TOMATO-GROWING SECRET!

Tomatoes need calcium. I firmly believe adequate soil calcium produces the best-tasting fruits, and I and several thousand other love apple lovers have discovered that calcium helps your plants avoid one of the biggest bummers experienced by tomato growers everywhere— blossom end rot. This heartbreak occurs when long wet spells, long dry spells, and/or alternating drought and flood (and lack of calcium in the soil) cause the fruit to go bad on the bottom, turning black at the heinie end and rotting out just as the tomato is ripening up.

So save up all your eggshells beginning around New Year. (Or make friends with somebody who works in a restaurant that serves breakfast). Let the fresh shells air-dry (just twenty-four hours or so and they're nice and crumbly), store them in their original containers (so you know how many a dozen is) and then add the crushed-up shells of a dozen or so eggs to each planting hole wherein you hope to achieve tomato happiness. (Cucumbers too, but for a different reason; it makes them crisper.)

I can assure you that this works *great*! In fact, its greatness has been personally reaffirmed year after year in my very own garden! I may have other things go wrong (and often do; I warned you that this was fun!), but since I became a born-again eggshell saver, my tomatoes have *never* had blossom end rot.

The season before I wrote the very first edition of this book, I had started to wonder if I had perhaps been fooling myself all these years, and if the Eggshell Thing *really* mattered. But I had saved *tons* of eggshells already, *and* it had been raining all spring, so I added a buncha crushed shells to each hole, and then it *really* started raining and never stopped. By August, everybody else's tomatoes looked *awful*—lots of blossom end rot—while mine were 100 percent rot-free and some of the nicest looking I'd ever grown. (I also spaced them farther away from each other and from other plants than usual that year.)

So air-dry the shells of a dozen eggs (they really do turn bone-dry in just a day or so), crush 'em up real fine, and mix 'em into the soil right around the roots of your tomatoes. Don't believe me? Try it with a few plants and leave the others shell-free. I guarantee you'll eat lots of eggs the winter after the results are in.

Tomatoes in Containers

Before you go this route, be honest with yourself. Will you be content with cherry tomatoes or the smallish fruit of paste, patio, or other determinate varieties? If the answer is yes, you may skip ahead to the next part of the test. But if the answer is "*No!* I want Brandywines, Big Boys, and Mortgage Lifters; I want tomatoes the size of a child's head!" you should first examine any other choices you have—because growing big tomatoes in containers is difficult. *Darned* difficult.

Could you possibly sharecrop with a gardening friend who wouldn't mind you putting a couple of plants in his garden ground? Or is there a community garden near your home or work where you could get—or share—a plot for the season? Either option would actually be *preferable* to containers no matter your tomato choice, as there would be other gardeners around to offer advice and teach you the tricks that will allow you to really hit the ground running when you have Earth-of-Your-Own.

Otherwise, you must *absolutely* buy *big* containers. I get good large tomato results in pots that are seventeen inches high and twenty inches across the top (450 by 500 millimeters). Yours don't have to be that *exact* size—anything close to it should be fine—but they *do* have to be *big*. You can grow things like peppers, eggplants, and cukes in smaller containers, but big tomatoes need a *lot* of room. And only *one* plant per pot, although you *can* grow other things in there as well.

Don't fall in love with containers that don't have drainage holes unless you're capable of drilling some yourself. ("*Crack*" goes the $40 pot!) Always check the bottoms of your containers; sometimes you'll have to drill holes, sometimes there are plugs that must be removed. And if the bottom of a container is very flat to the ground, put it up on bricks so the holes don't become obstructed.

Unglazed terra cotta pots look great, but their porosity wicks the water from your soil right out into the air. Plants in such pots often need to be watered every day—sometimes several times a day—and are practically guaranteed to die of drought when you go on vacation. Terra cotta is also breakable, heavy, and can't be left outdoors over winter. (Well, that's not *quite* true; you *can* leave them out. They'll just crack.) *Plastic* pots are lighter, less expensive, retain moisture better, laugh at winter, and come in a huge variety of sizes and colors—including my favorite: fake terra cotta. If you're just *stone* in love with terra cotta, find plastic pots that are slightly smaller and slip them inside, where they won't be seen.

As with seed starting, don't fill these containers with lousy, weedy, outside dirt; it's darned near impossible to keep plants alive in that stuff

When you see the term **Patio Tomato**, you can be sure you're getting a compact plant designed for growth in containers. The plant's fruit will never have the complex flavors or monster size of some heirloom varieties, but you won't have kudzu-like vines pushing your outdoor furniture out of the way, either. Patio tomatoes tend to produce a good number of medium-sized tomatoes for salads and slicing and are an excellent choice for those who want to be certain their plant will be well behaved.

outdoors in a garden, much less than when they're imprisoned in a pot. Find a nice soil-free potting mix; these lightweight blends of natural substances like peat, perlite, and vermiculite are available at virtually all garden centers (just avoid the ones laced with nasty chemical fertilizers). Then mix some nice yard-waste compost—yours, bagged or bulk—in with the potting soil: about one-quarter compost and three-quarters mix.

Note: Some premium potting soils contain *natural* nutrients like worm castings—these are better than fine; they are ideal. Some may also contain added trace minerals that are highly beneficial to plants and otherwise hard to find. You hit the jackpot when you use one of these high-end organic soil-free mixes! Just say no to chemical fertilizers, water-holding crystals, and other *unnatural* elements.

Do not put peanuts, pebbles, old car batteries, broken pot shards, or other similar items in the bottom. That old "improve the drainage" fallacy has long since been disproved. Your plants want to be able to send their roots through soil (actually soil-free mix) all the way down to the bottom of the pot, and having a bunch of junk down there *worsens* the results rather than improves them.

Find a spot for your pots that gets morning sun, lots of sun, is out in the open with great airflow, and where water will be able to drain freely out the bottoms. Remember, if your containers fit a little too flush to the ground, prop them up on a few bricks; water *must* be able to drain freely out the bottom. Carry the empty pots to that spot and fill them up there. Even a lightweight mix can become heavy in pots that size, and it's better to fill them up in place than try and move them around. Oh, and don't bother buying saucers for underneath; you *don't* want water to sit down there—all it can do is drown your plants and breed mosquitoes.

To get the most out of your pots, use them to grow cool-weather crops like lettuce and other salad greens early in the season—before you could safely put out your tomatoes. Set the pots up on the first nice day, water the mix well, spread the seeds of a nice leaf lettuce or salad green mix overtop, cover the seeds with a thin layer of potting mix, and mist it well. Cover the top at night with clear plastic to retain heat, but take the plastic off during the day. Spritz the surface daily and the lettuce should sprout in about five or six days. No more plastic after that.

Let the lettuce grow until it's three or four inches (75 or 100 millimeters) high and then begin to harvest it with scissors "cut and come again" style, mostly from around the edges, letting the plants in the middle grow. The cut lettuce will regrow, and you should be able to make several harvests before tomato-planting time arrives. Then, harvest the center plants completely and install your tomato, following the advice of burying the stem deeply and adding eggshells. Continue to harvest the "outside" lettuce until it turns bitter (you'll see a white liquid when you cut the leaves at this point), then replace it with trailing nasturtiums (for spicy good eating) or compact herbs or even some small flowers just to make things look nice. Again, only one *tomato* plant per pot, but feel free to plant a ring of smallish things around it.

And finally, be aware that in addition to buying pots that look like they belong outside a hotel, you'll have to enclose the sprawling plants in full-sized tomato cages made of welded-wire animal fencing (which we will discuss in the very next chapter).

If you want (or need) to utilize slightly smaller pots, grow bush-style determinate plants; they can get by with the support provided by a large store-bought tomato cage or similar structure.

Sun Gold

Sun Gold is the favored tiny tomato of many gardeners. The beautiful little tomatoes come on fast and are often the first in the garden to ripen—generally even before varieties with "early" in their name! These yellowish-orange treats have a unique citrus-like flavor.

Chapter 4

Staking and Caging

(And no, that's not staking *or* caging. It's staking *and* caging!)

Unsupported tomato vines will crawl along the ground, where slugs and other dastardly creatures will take one big bite (and only one) out of each of your love apples, ruining the harvest and your chance for a happy life.

Yes, it's time to stake *and* cage those teeny-tiny plants of yours *despite* their current teeny-tininess. Because they aren't gonna stay teeny-tiny for long.

Yes—you *have* to stake AND cage. For two reasons:

1) Tomatoes are vines. Or rather, tomatoes (the fruit) grow on vines (henceforth known as "the plants"). Either way, they ain't trees. Left to their own devices, your tomato plants will just flop right down onto the soil. And their lying prone on the ground like that makes it impossible for the plants to get good air circulation, thus making them very susceptible to diseases. And the fruit will just plain rot if it's touching wet ground. It'll get all dirty, too.

That's why most people *at least* stake their tomatoes. They drive a six- or eight-foot (2- or 2.5-meter) stake deep into the ground, leaving only four to six feet (1 to 2 meters) aboveground, and then gently (and continually, as the plant grows) secure the main tomato vine to that stake with something that won't cut into the vine and sever it under pressure (*not*, for example, fishing line or piano wire—although such choices *do* speed us toward the end of this movie a *lot* faster).

Caging

To give your tomatoes proper air circulation, keep them safe from disease, and prevent them from taking over your garden, you need to stake and cage each tomato plant.

But I'm *not* recommending that you live by the stake—in fact, I'm against it. Because the tying-the-rapidly-developing-vine-to-a-stake thing, she no work. Nope—remember how I said the vines of the best-tasting tomatoes grow twelve to fourteen feet (3.5 to 4 meters) long? And we got, what—maybe five feet (1.5 meters) of stake above ground? Heck, even I can do the math on that one! Luckily, people who try this unworkable technique generally don't get to the point where there's more vine than stake to worry about. No, long before that, they'll be out there trying to tie up some rogue limb, carefully lift it into position, and hear that heart-breaking *snap!* that means "you have now killed this plant; *and* it's too late in the season to replace it."

I don't even advise staking shorter determinate varieties. First, you have to find that magic material that can hold a ten- to twenty-pound (4.5- to 10-kilogram) cluster of fruit steadily without cutting into the vine. *And* you have to remember to constantly keep up with the new growth during the season.

Now, we *are* going to *use* stakes. But we're going to use *our* stakes to hold our *cages* in place.

2) Your plants are growing all summer. As mentioned previously, your little plants that are now just inches tall will grow like the dickens and become very tall. And gangly. Remember: The vines of a big heirloom tomato plant (like Brandywine, Jefferson Giant, Georgia Streak, Mortgage Lifter, etc.) can reach fourteen feet (4 meters) in length. And while we *do* want lots of airflow around the leaves, we probably also want to grow a few other plants in this garden, so these giants need to be *contained* as well as supported.

So what we're gonna do is surround these teeny-tiny, barely visible little plants with a *big honkin' cage.* And we're gonna support that cage with a nice sturdy six-foot (2-meter) stake, driven a couple of feet into the ground through the holes in the material of the cage. The stake will prevent the cage from falling over in high winds and heavy rains, and also from being dragged down by the overwhelming weight and size of the fully grown plant loaded with the pounds and pounds and pounds of fruit that will soon be drooping and pulling all over it.

Anyway, while tomatoes are not pumpkins (the true three hundred–pound gorillas of the garden), some of the big heirlooms come darn close.

And a well-supported cage overcomes the height problem (twelve-foot vine; five-foot stake) by taking advantage of the fact that tomato vines do *not* grow straight up, but kind of slouch and roll around the edges—like teenagers, their posture is poor. So the plant will curl around the sides

Fishing line and piano wire are exceptionally poor choices for tying up tomatoes. Twist ties can be risky as well, because they have wire inside. Strips of soft cloth or foam or a commercial "tie-your-tomatoes-up" product are much better. But better still would be to reject this foolish path and instead "cage 'em and forget 'em."

It's very difficult to find a material that will hold your tomato plant to a stake without destroying it. That is why you should use stakes to support your tomato cages rather than the plants themselves.

> To contain your tomatoes, you need a cage. As Carl Denham proved in that Broadway show he did with the big gorilla from Skull Island back in the 30s, chains are simply not enough—even "chains made of chromed steel."

somewhat as it slowly climbs up the inside of the cage as it grows, using up a lot of its growth in sideways motion. By the time a typical big vine reaches the top of even a five foot (1.5 meter)-high cage, it's probably used up a good eight or nine feet (3 meters) of its own personal length. Then, even the longest vine can spill over the top of the cage, grow back down along the outside, and still *not* touch the ground before frost puts this show to bed for the season. (If the tip of an *enormously* long vine grown this way *should* reach the ground, you can: a) trim the new growth off; b) train the vine over to the next cage; c) tie the vine sideways to a relatively open section of the cage; or d) run screaming for the hills in fear.

Let us now pause for a word about those premade conical three foot (1 meter)-high "tomato cages" sold in hardware stores and garden centers in the spring:

HA!

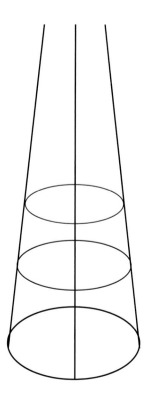

Those are not cages, my friend. If we define a "cage" as being something like the structures that prevent leopards at the zoo from having the visitors for breakfast, then these wittle bitty things are jars with holes in the lids for catching lightning bugs on a hot summer night.

Now, I actually own some of those kinds of tomato cages. I use them to support big-fruited bell pepper plants like California Wonder and Fat & Sassy and classic big eggplants. But to use one of them pitiful little things to support a *tomato* plant would be like trying to tow a truck with kite string.

Making Cages

Simply put, you probably won't find a sturdy enough structure for sale ready-made. But you *will* find what you need to make such structures—probably right at the same place that you couldn't find the ready-made one.

You want to buy a roll of *sturdy* five or six foot (1.5 or 2 meter)-high, welded-wire *fencing. Not* chicken wire. You can make a darn good compost bin out of chicken wire. You can also roll chicken wire out flat on the fluffy, loose soil of your raised beds to deter kitty cats who are mistaking those beds for litter boxes. You can seed crops like lettuce and spinach and such right through the flattened fencing, and use tin snips to cut holes in it for the insertion of tomato and pepper transplants and the like—works great! But you can't use it to cage tomatoes. It's not rigid enough, and you can't reach through the tiny little openings to pick your tomatoes and/or to pick slugs and/or hornworms off your tomatoes.

The fencing you use needs to be sturdy *and* have big enough openings that you can squeeze a hand through when necessary. Those openings don't have to be large enough to pass your future tomatoes through, especially if you're growing big ones. You probably will be able to "direct pick" paste and cherry tomatoes, but for most of the big boys you'll have to reach down over the sides for them; or if they're really low, hand them up the inside of the fencing like a ballpark hot dog.

Any large hardware store or garden center will have a good variety of choices. They may be labeled animal fencing, rabbit fencing, turkey wire, or the like. Concrete reinforcing wire is a little over-the-top (as in more support than you need, even for Mortgage Lifters), but it gets rave reviews from folks who've used it, and the openings are big enough to pass a Brandywine through.

These materials come in rolls that are typically twenty-five, fifty, or one hundred feet (8, 15, or 30 meters) long. The hundred-foot (30-meter) rolls can get pretty heavy, so I generally buy fifty foot (15 meter)-long rolls, from which you can make eight to ten cages. I bought a couple of fifty-foot rolls of fairly generic animal/rabbit fencing for about twenty bucks a roll over two decades ago, and the cages I made from it are still in great shape. However, I eventually retired them from tomato growing (they now hold fall leaves and compost-makings) when I found something really spiffy to use instead. (OK—and because some of them got a little rusty over the years.)

It's called Gard'n Fence (yes, I saved the wrapper!). It's made in Italy, is five feet (1.5 meters) high, comes in a fifty-foot (15-meter) roll, and has two-by-three-inch (50-by-75-millimeter) openings in the mesh, which are a *little* small for my hands, but the fencing is nicely flexible, so I can easily bend a little extra into the top and bottom of a section and then squeeze my hand through to pick and/or pass the ripe tomatoes out. In a pinch, I can also make a double door by cutting between two sections with tin snips. I was first attracted to this roll of fencing because of the color—a beautiful dark green. The fencing itself is actually metal, but it's coated with a layer of green vinyl, which means it won't rust like my old cages (or maybe it will, but we won't see it because the rust would be under the green vinyl coating). It looked like it would make really nice tomato cages in the store, and it certainly has. If you flip back to page 67, you can see one of the tomato cages I made using this fabulous stuff.

I made nine cages out of the roll. All are still in use (it must be twelve years later at this point), and all were cut to be somewhat different in size, which I strongly urge you to do as well.

I *used* to make all my cages from six-foot (2-meter) lengths of fencing, which *is* an ideal size. But it makes them hard to store at the end of the season, unless you undo what's holding them in a circle and lay them out flat, which is work, which I avoid. So with *this* roll, I made a couple cages out of six foot (2 meter)-long sections, some out of five and a half foot (1.7 meter)-long sections, and then the final ones were made from five-foot (1.5-meter) lengths of fencing. Start to keep track of what's left when you've got, say, six cages done so you don't end up with a short section from which you could only make a giant spitball tube.

My biggest heirloom plants go into the six-footers (which have a finished diameter of around twenty-two or twenty-three inches [600 millimeters]), my compact paste tomato varieties go into the smallest cages (five-foot [1.5-meter] lengths, a diameter of seventeen to eighteen inches [450 millimeters]), and then I attempt to predict final tomato plant sizes to fit what's left. At the end of the season, you can slide a five-footer inside a five-and-a-halfer and then slide them both inside a six-footer—like those Russian doll thingies.

BIG SPACE-SAVING TIP

When you make your tomato cages, vary them enough in initial length of fencing so when the season is over you can stack two smaller ones inside each really big one. That way, there's a prayer they won't eat up your meager storage space.

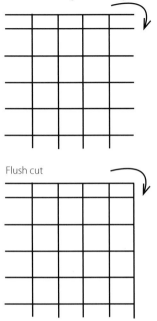

Cut for attaching to flush edge

Flush cut

HOW TO MAKE TOMATO CAGES

Get a helper, a good pair of leather gloves for each of you, and a pair of tin snips. Do the work on a nice flat surface, like a driveway.

Measure out six linear feet (2 meters) (or another length of your choice) of fencing, have your helper hold it down/out, and cut it off the roll with tin snips so the newly-cut-from-the-roll end will have loose pieces of fencing material sticking out along the cut edge. The edge of what's left on the roll should be flush, like the end of the roll itself before you started. This part is important; look at the pictures at the left. You want to be sure and cut it this way because those stuck-out spokes on your cut section are the "attached twist ties" you're going to use to hold your cage together in a circle.

Now shape your piece of cut fencing into a circle and use those natural, twist tie–like spokes to attach one side to the other—just wrap them around the edges of the little openings on the flush side until they're nice and secure and then flatten them sideways against the cage so no sharp edges are protruding. This will give you a much more secure structure than if you tried to use string, wire, twist ties, or telekinesis to hold the edges together. *Your* connectors are part of the actual fencing, and there's nothing stronger.

A well-built tomato cage keeps your ever-expanding tomato plant in a contained space. And, if you make yourself a set of homemade cages this season, you'll probably be able to hang onto them for years to come.

Photo by Fox Chapel Publishing.

Now look at the bottom of the fencing. (Which end is the bottom? Your choice! *You* decide which end will rest in the dirt and which shall strain toward the sky! Don't abuse this awesome power.) It should be one nice continuous piece of wire fencing stuff. Not for long. Take your tin snips and cut one side of the very bottom of every third or fourth little rectangular opening (*not* all of them—just a few of them, evenly spaced) so you can straighten out each of those little still-attached pieces of wire and point them downward, making little positioning stakes.

Now position your assembled cage so that the ridiculously small tomato you expect to become the biggest honking plant of all time come July is in the center. If you want to use a cutworm collar, put it on there now; see "Block That Pest!" on page 73. Shove the cage into the ground so those little stakes you made in the bottom go all the way into the soil. Now remove the cage for a second and cover the area between the plant and those little holes in the soil with your mulch of choice, which should be compost or one of the options listed in "Your Mulch Choices" on page 74. Then put the cage into place for real.

Now take a six-foot (2-meter) stake, a long piece of rebar, or some other such stake-like item, and position it through an opening in the cage, about three feet (900 millimeters) up from the ground (best to place it in the *back* of the cage, where it will be behind the tomato plant when the plant is full-grown and thus hidden from view) and pound it with a sledgehammer down a good two feet (600 millimeters) into the ground. Then, when it (or you) will be pounded no more, either walk away looking capable, or secure it to the cage with wire or heavy-duty twist ties. I personally just walk away.

You've done it! You've caged a tomato! It won't get away now!

Now continue making cages out of the rest of the roll. The exact sizes are up to you—and depend, of course, on what kind of plants you'll be growing. If they're all going to be *big* heirlooms (and cage storage isn't an issue), just make eight big ones, each using a smidge more than six feet (2 meters) of fencing. All compact paste tomatoes? Make ten five-footers (1.5 meters) out of that fifty-foot (15-meter) roll.

A final word on parenting/tomatoing: Caging and staking your young, tiny tomatoes is like reading to your children before they're old enough to possibly understand anything you're saying. It may look foolish to others, but it gets your loved ones off to a great start.

USING FIFTY FEET OF WIRE

If you're compulsive and need a finite plan, here's a good one to use an entire fifty-foot (15-meter) roll of wire:

- 4 cages made using 6′ (2m) lengths = 24′ (7m) of fencing
- 2 cages made using 5½′ (1.7m) lengths = 11′ (3m) of fencing
- 3 cages made using 5′ (1.5m) lengths = 15′ (5m) of fencing

Total: Nine cages made using all fifty feet (15 meters) of fencing

Ta da! Amazing! (I think this is actually pretty much what I did that year.)

The cutworm is shown here in its egg, larva, and pupa stages.

A Few Words about Cutworms

It has never happened to me personally, but I've heard from many gardeners who *have* suffered the heartbreak of *Cutwormariasus*. You come out to the garden one bright and hopeful morning early in the season and your young tomato transplants (and other garden crops as well) are lying on their sides, separated cleanly from their life-sustaining roots, which are still stuck tight in the soil.

The nasty larval form of a useless but otherwise harmless moth, cutworms are the worst kind of garden pests. My insect specialist buddy, Dr. Linda Gilkeson, describes the cutworm as "a fat, greasy caterpillar" in *Rodale's Pest & Disease Problem Solver* (one of those books that allows you to look up in wretched living color all the creatures and diseases that have eaten and/or infected your garden). Cutworms kill only young plants—i.e., your beautiful, wonderful, hope-for-the-future transplants of spring. Perhaps even more insulting, they don't even eat them! At least not right away. Apparently, cutworms sever transplants at the soil line so the young plants will topple over and the vile, greasy little creature can later consume them without much effort. This slacker tactic of plant predation may work well in the wild, but in the home garden setting, all it does is crush the hopes and shatter the dreams of countless novice gardeners each year, as they discover their young charges leveled one morning.

If what appears to be cutworm damage strikes, snoop around the scene of the crime. You will probably find a cutworm or two (or twenty) curled up next to a severed plant or just under the surface of the soil. Feel free to exact revenge if you do. But 'tis better to avoid this problem up front by using cutworm collars when you plant. You should especially consider doing so if:

- your young transplants have suffered such damage in the past;
- you're planting a garden for the first time, don't know what to expect, and want to be careful (I think insurance is always worth it);
- you didn't freshly till the soil, double dig it, or otherwise cultivate it before planting (doing so exposes the cutworms to wonderfully hungry birds); or
- I've made you so paranoid that you won't be able to sleep otherwise.

So I'M A CUTWORM YOU GOT A PROBLEM WITH THAT?

BLOCK THAT PEST!

It's really easy to thwart cutworms. Just make a circle of relatively hard material and shove it into the dirt around the young transplant. Your established options include:

- **Tin cans without lid or bottom.** Remove both ends of a soup (or similarly sized) can and insert the metal cylinder over the transplant, sinking it one or two inches (25 or 50 millimeters) into the soil.

- **A plastic soda bottle.** Cut the top and bottom off of a one- or two-liter bottle and use as described previously.

- **Magazine "blow in" direct response cards.** Open up any new copy of any magazine, allow the six hundred or so little cards inserted therein to drop onto your lap, select the biggest ones, fold them over into circles, and use as above. If, however, you catch the cutworms filling out the cards and trying to subscribe to, say, Prevention or Bug's Health, quickly move your family to another state.

Don't worry—growing tomatoes is like raising children: Perfection on your part is simply not possible. You're going to screw up, but they'll probably be just fine anyway as long as you tried your best.

Just like the name implies, **Lemon Boy** tomatoes are yellow. This is an indeterminate variety, so it will need lots of room to grow, but you'll be rewarded with tons of tasty, meaty tomatoes.

Your Mulch Choices

You want to surround your young transplants with something that will prevent weed growth and retain soil moisture before you cage them, and your best choice is *compost!*

Two inches (50 millimeters) of high-quality compost:

- prevent weeds just as well as two inches (50 millimeters) of nasty, disease-cultivating shredded bark, chipped wood, or other nasty no-goodnik wood mulch (Three universities—Ohio State, Iowa State, and the University of Kentucky—say so; no universities say otherwise; and yes, nasty wood mulch *is* nasty!);
- provide all the food your young tomato plants will need for quite some time, in a form they really like;
- prevent disease better than anything you can spray. Compost creates an actual, physical barrier against the ground-level breeding of disease spores; wood mulches breed disease, and do so *very* well.

And compost avoids the number one argument against mulching: slugs! In a wet and shady area (or season), slugs can become an intolerable garden pest. There are many ways to fight them: beer, sharp sticks, diatomaceous earth, salt, copper, vinegar, small-caliber handguns, and the laying down of boards as traps. But cutting back on mulch can also be a *huge* help. Now don't get me wrong—a thick layer of weed-suppressing, moisture-conserving, soil-cooling mulch is one of the basic tenets of organic gardening. Unfortunately, most mulches also give slugs a place to hide during the day. So if, like *moi*, you must garden in a sun-challenged site and/or a region where perpetual moistness be the norm, forgo any mulch other than compost.

However, the rest of you—especially those who garden in full sun and/or in a really hot locale, and *especially* where it generally doesn't rain—can use any non-wood mulch instead. Although it won't prevent disease, two inches (50 millimeters) of shredded leaves will prevent weeds, retain soil moisture, and attract earthworms that will feed your plants with their wonderful *castings*.

Use shredded leaves (Not *whole* ones! Really! Whole leaves mat down like a wet tarp), *dried* (not green) grass clippings from a chemical-free lawn (if herbicides were used, then *do not use the clippings!*), straw (*not* hay!), pine straw (luckily, there is no pine hay), or seed or nut hull mulches.

Don't mulch directly against the stem of the plant; begin about three inches (75 millimeters) away from the stem all the way out to the edge of the cage in a layer no more than two inches (50 millimeters) deep.

But for disease-prone plants like tomatoes, there is really no other choice than compost, which will also feed your plants brilliantly, *and* a two-inch (50-millimeter) layer of compost on top of the soil around your plants is the *best* hedge against disease. Apply a fresh half-inch (15 millimeters) or so of compost every two months afterward during the growing season (and promptly remove and destroy any discolored leaves) and you will prevent many problems.

Oh, and don't let all this disease talk scare you. Sure, tomatoes *are* more prone to plant diseases here where their leaves get wet than in their native dry clime, but you're going to do just fine.

Fourth of July. This variety's name promises the Holy Grail of tomato growing—ripe red fruit by the Fourth of July. In most areas of the country, it's not easy to achieve this legendary bragging right, as most plants take much longer than the allotted time to produce ripe fruit. To celebrate the Fourth in love apple style, you need to start your plants early, protect the young plants with hot caps or cloches early in the season, and of course, choose a variety whose days to maturity—and perhaps its very name—leans right into your expectations.

Chapter 5

Food, Water, and Basic Keeping-Alive Skills

(Oops—you mean I *shouldn't* have watered them each and every day?)

If you've come even remotely close to doing what we've suggested thus far, the next couple of months should be a breeze. This really *is* like house painting, where the actual time spent slapping the paint on seems infinitesimal compared to the hours and hours of laborious cleaning and prep work that you did beforehand. And if you've done *everything* we've suggested, the only real purpose of this chapter will be to warn you not to overwater. Really. I firmly believe that people trying to do too much kills more tomatoes than bugs and blights combined. *They're plants, people! Not premature babies!*

Seriously, if you got your plants off to a good start, buried 'em deep, fed 'em eggshells, mixed some compost into their loosened-up soil and/or spread some on top of their already good soil, gave 'em plenty of air space, mulched 'em well, and all that other stuff you didn't do, you can just kick back for the next couple of months. Unless drought strikes. Then you have to wake up and water.

Oh, and I guess I should tell you exactly how to do that watering. And you probably want to know what to feed them, too, so…

Opalka

Large for a paste tomato (a much sought after attribute by us saucers), the uniquely (some say banana) shaped fruit of the **Opalka** tomato is very meaty. This popular heirloom variety is great for sandwiches and especially good for faster processing of tomato sauce and paste. A nice conversation starter in the garden as well.

"Feeding" Your Tomatoes

Like that guy in *The Graduate*, I got one word for you (and it ain't "plastic"). It's *compost*.

Way back in Chapter 3, I urged you to mix some compost in with your soil when you loosened it up and/or to spread some compost on the surface of your previously prepared soil. If you did so heed me and utilized this priceless (actually you can buy it pretty cheap) soil amendment, you really don't need to feed your plants anything else for a while. And if you wish to remain pure, you can just continue to feed 'em more compost throughout the season. If, however, you *only* loosened up your soil (or even worse, just plunged your poor plants into pretty much un-amended rock-hard clay or super-porous sand), then you need to add some compost right now.

If you're reading this before the actual planting process and you don't expect disease to be a significant problem (because you haven't grown tomatoes in this spot before, the spot gets morning sun, you have enough garden space to ensure good airflow between the fully grown plants, and you have a history of being fatally optimistic), you can go ahead and mix some of the compost into the soil before you start planting.

How much? Ideally, an amount that would equal a one- to two-inch (25- to 50-millimeter) layer on top of about a two-by-two-foot (600-by-600-millimeter) plot of soil (my approximation of the "footprint" of the average full-grown tomato plant). If you feel the need to measure *something*, spread out an inch or two (25 to 50 millimeters) of compost on top of a two-by-two-foot (600-by-600-millimeter) area in the center of which you shall soon plant. Then mix it up with the soil that's already there (minus rocks and clay clods, of course).

If the plant is already in the ground, spread two inches (50 millimeters) of compost all around it, covering that two-by-two-foot (600-by-600-millimeter) area (feel free to extend it out even further for really big plants). If you're in the crowd that mixed some compost into the soil previously, spread another inch (25 millimeters) on top—two inches (50 millimeters) would be better. Compost used as a mulch prevents weeds just as well as shredded bark or wood chips (both of which breed disease and are *bad* for plants), provides all the foods our growing plants need, and prevents disease spores from breeding on the surface of the soil (wood and bark mulches *encourage* such sinister spores—did I mention that wood mulches are bad?).

Compost is unbeatable; we're talking the King *and* Queen of garden nutrients!

That's right—I want you to place compost down *on top of* the soil, even if you already mixed compost *into* the soil itself. That layer of compost is like a force field against disease.

COMPOST TEA

Now, I'm a realist. I *know* you have a burning desire to feed and nurture your plants throughout the season. And I apologize for revealing the harsh reality that you probably don't need to, generally shouldn't, and that *truly* unbridled kindness at the plant food trough will kill your big green buddies more surely than a sledgehammer.

But I know you feel like you *have* to do *something*. So here's a safe way to feed your need without overfeeding your plants: Brew up some compost tea once a month or so during the season. It's fun, it can be really messy (see "fun"), your plants will love it, and perhaps most important, it will provide you with something mysterious to do in public that your neighbors can point to and whisper guesses about and that you can later tell them is your secret for growing those beautiful tomatoes (besides the egg shells).

Place some nice, finished compost into a porous cloth container (an old sock for a gallon [4 liters] of water; a tied-up old t-shirt for a five-gallon [19-liter] bucket of water, or an old pillowcase for a big [clean!] trash can full of water). Place this "tea bag" in the container of your choice, fill it with cool water, let it steep in the shade for twenty-four hours, and—voilà! You've got compost tea.

When it's done steeping, remove the bag and return the contents of the bag to your compost pile. Thin the liquid with water until it's the color of tea (if you followed those precise measurements of mine correctly, the initial result should have been the color of coffee), and then use it to water your plants—*quickly*! Compost tea is full of living beneficial organisms and they're using up the limited amount of oxygen in that water. So make only what you'll need (or use all you make—any plant would love a drink of this stuff) within an hour or so of tea-bag removal time.

Since morning is the best time to water your plants, start your tea brewing around 10 a.m. on Saturday morning and use it around 10 or 11 a.m. Sunday morning; you'll deliver the maximum number of beneficial soil helpers to the roots of your precious plants.

I know you don't believe me when I say you shouldn't feed your plants, so feel free to ignore my sage advice (go ahead and side with my family! I knew you were against me!). But if you do feed your plants every two weeks like a certain actor-turned-chemical-salesman tells you to on TV, they'll look like you would if you ate a triple-size burger and fries three times a day.

Compost Alternatives

Come on—compost is The Best. You can't make some compost? You don't know *anybody* who can "loan" you some compost? Your township doesn't make compost from all of your fall leaves and then give it away (actually "back") to people like you? Local nurseries don't sell it in bulk? You can't find a bag of compost for sale at *any* local garden center?

The simple truth of garden nutrition is that compost *really* is number one, and it's a *long* drive down to number two.

MANURE

When thinking about using manure as plant food, take the Elmer Fudd warning and "be vewy, vewy careful." While garden lore, advice from old codgers ("my tomatoes had to walk six miles to get to school! Uphill! Both ways!"), and other methods of misinformation would have you believe that manure is good, it often isn't. *And* there is no single such thing *as* "manure."

Here are some manure rules and realities:

1) Never put "raw" or "fresh" manure on your garden! It stinks, it can be full of pathogens, it stinks, it can be full of weed seeds just waiting to sprout (especially horse manure), it stinks, and it could "burn" your plants with its excess nitrogen. Smells bad, too.

2) Composted manures *may* be OK. *Composted* manure—the result of piling up the stuff the animal was done with and the bedding that such stuff fell into—has no objectionable odor, is cool to the touch, and looks like dark soil or compost.

3) Even composted, horse or poultry manure is not for fruiting plants. Yes, I know that hundreds of people have told you, "oh, just give your plants some horse manure!" Those hundreds of people are either wrong, just plain evil, or want to make sure you don't get nearly as many tomatoes as they do. Horse and poultry manure are excessively rich in nitrogen, the nutrient that makes plants grow real big real fast. But nitrogen can also inhibit flowering, which is why people who fall for the horse manure trap often end up with huge tall plants with two tomatoes on them. *Composted* (always composted!) horse manure and poultry manure are excellent for feeding non-fruiting plants, like sweet corn and lawns, but are a poor choice for flowers and other garden crops we grow for their fruit—like tomatoes, peppers, eggplants, zucchini, etc. If the thing you want to eat replaces a flower on the plant, don't feed the plant horse or poultry manure.

4) Composted cow manure is theoretically much safer. It's a "cold" manure (not a lot of nitrogen—or anything else really) and its (relatively weak) nutrients are balanced. But like I've already gently implied here, there ain't

much plant-growing octane in cow manure's tank—and sadly, the manure probably came from animals that were crowded, confined, over-medicated, and fed artificial hormones that make me nervous as hell. (Most of the human cancers we can't seem to slow down and get under control are hormonal in nature, and we feed artificial hormones to the animals we eat?)

5) Now if you have access to manure from animals raised without hormones, continuous antibiotics, or psychotic confinement, you *can* use it. Mix some horse or poultry manure into your compost piles—or heck, just into big piles of shredded fall leaves—and you'll make super-excellent compost; *hot* compost—the most disease-fighting kind! (Same with cow manure, but it's much harder for regular humans to collect than the other two.) I might even add a small amount of *conventional composted* manure to a pile; the composting process can "cook" a lot of nasties out of the finished mix, and you'll be composting it a second time in your pile.

6) Llama poop, sheep poop, gerbil poop, rabbit poop—any poop from an animal that doesn't eat meat and that isn't routinely medicated—makes great food for your garden. I always like to mix such stuff in with my cooking compost, but in a pinch you could spread some of the poopy pellets around your plants—just be sure to cover them with some soil or compost afterward.

7) Sorry, but the waste from dogs and cats should *not* be used anywhere near a garden. Even indoor-only animals can harbor worms or parasites, and their waste should be carefully disposed of in the trash. I wish it were otherwise, but your pet's poop should never go into a garden or compost pile. Ever, ever, ever. Same for any other meat eater with soft feet or paws.

8) Elephant poop is fine. Circuses often give it away. The "pellets" are the size of footballs and so it's a little slow to break down, but spread some elephant poop in your patch and the deer will move to another state.

These still-slightly-green, herbicide-free grass clippings are almost ready to use as food and mulch.

Granular organic fertilizers should always be covered with some soil or compost to become active. Conventional ones too—but you're not going to do that because you're not a bad person. Anymore.

GRASS CLIPPINGS

Another treacherous entry. The good news: Research has shown that the dried clippings from an herbicide-free lawn are a tremendously good source of nutrients—well-balanced, even! And, as we said earlier, dried clippings from an herbicide-free lawn are one of the absolute best mulches for keeping down weeds as well.

The bad news: The clippings *must* come from a lawn that has *not* been treated with herbicides. Clippings from herbicide-treated lawns can kill garden plants when used as mulch. In fact, some of the nasty, dangerous lawn herbicides in use today can even survive the composting process. Compost made from treated clippings has been shown to kill plants in many studies and unfortunate real-life situations. So if you're not *certain* of your clippings' provenance, don't take the risk.

And they *must* be dried. Green clippings are too "hot" (nitrogen rich) and can burn plants. And green clippings mat down into a wet, green, slimy mess.

Plus, if you use a mulching mower with a sharp blade to return those clippings to your lawn in a super-pulverized form, it provides half the food your lawn needs in a season. So it's always better to let mulched clippings lie; there are many other potential fertilizers in the sea! (In fact, that's where one of the *best* fertilizers resides—or used to until they bottled it up for you.)

PACKAGED FERTILIZERS

If it's organic (says "approved for use in organic agriculture" or "certified organic" or "Organic Materials Review Institute [OMRI] approved" somewhere on the package), it's likely to be OK.

Liquid mixtures of fish and seaweed are my favorite mid-season boost fertilizers. They provide a great balance of the big essential nutrients, and the seaweed (or kelp; the terms are used interchangeably) component is full of trace elements and other hard-to-find nutrients that help plants better resist stress. Seaweed/kelp can even give plants a couple extra degrees of frost/cold weather endurance! Be wary of fish emulsion alone; these products are traditionally very high in nitrogen and some contain way too much chlorine.

Granulated fertilizers (again, organically approved ones) are fine, but use them sparingly, don't let the granules touch the stem of any plants, and always cover granular fertilizers with a little soil or compost after you apply them (it activates the nutrients faster).

Avoid overly strong fertilizers—and unbalanced ones like the foolishly popular 10-10-10 fertilizer, which is both too strong *and* unbalanced. I know the *numbers* are equal, but no plant on the planet uses the "big three" nutrients in equal amounts.

Like it says in "Solving the NPK Mystery!" below, the ideal ratio of nutrients for fruiting plants like tomatoes is 3-1-2 (or, as my old friend Cheryl Long used to call it, "the ratio that no dyslexic can ever remember").

Now, if you want to try and induce a little more flowering (and thus fruit), bonemeal is the best source of fairly immediate phosphorus (the P in NPK—the middle number on a bag of fertilizer), which is *the* essential nutrient for getting lots of flowers and fruit. Bonemeal makes its phosphorus available faster than any other P source, so it would be the bloom booster you'd use at the beginning of the season. Rock phosphate (a mined mineral product) is much better but takes much longer to become available—you'd have to apply rock phosphate (just a little; it's highly concentrated) the fall *before*. Whatever you use, spread some soil or compost over top to get it working a little faster.

Bonemeal, rich in phosphorus, is a fertilizer that encourages flowering; and more flowers = more fruit.

SOLVING THE NPK MYSTERY!

Take a look at any packaged fertilizer. Organic or chemical, powdered, granular, or liquid, it will have a set of three numbers displayed prominently on the label, like 10-10-10 (bad), 5-3-5 (better, but far from ideal), or 3-1-2 (perfect). Those numbers are that fertilizer's NPK ratio—the relative amounts of Nitrogen (N), Phosphorus (P), and Potassium (K) the fertilizer contains. Based on all the available evidence, it appears that a ratio of 3-1-2 is ideal for most garden plants. Here's a little NPK 101:

Nitrogen (N): Nitrogen is the basic plant food—it helps grow a big, strong "body" and lots of leaves. But feeding plants that you want to produce lots of flowers and/or fruit too much of this nutrient can limit the amount of flowers and fruit because the plant is putting too much energy into making lush, leafy green growth instead of producing fruit. You will note that in our ideal 3-1-2 world, nitrogen is still the dominant nutrient. That's because nitrogen is ephemeral; it moves around so much in the soil and is so quickly taken up and used by plants that it needs to be replaced more often than the other nutrients.

Phosphorus (P): As far as I'm concerned, this is *the* key nutrient for top tomato production. It helps plants put down strong roots and encourages them to produce more flowers, which on tomato plants

Some folks worry that you might catch mad cow disease from bonemeal because it's made from cow bones. Others say that all the nutrition's been cooked away. And others fear that it will attract squirrels that will uproot the plants. I use it and get lots of tomatoes.

MAD-TOMATO DISEASE

turn into, well…tomatoes. Because it *is* essential to strong root growth, you want this puppy to be in the soil right away. It's OK to add a little nitrogen later in the season if you suffer from Puny Plants; you need your P to be there from day one. And it has to be right where the roots can reach it—phosphorus doesn't travel in the soil like nitrogen. That's why I'll often toss a handful of bonemeal into each planting hole—right on top of the old eggshells. Rock phosphate is *the best* source of P, but your soil has to be nice and acidic and alive for it to work its best. A product called colloidal rock phosphate is almost as P rich, but a *lot* less needy, and it's especially good for use in sandy soils—it's a little "clayey" and it helps hold the sand particles together better. Either way, a little goes a long way, and it needs a fairly long time to become active and available to your plants. But it also lasts a long time; you should only add rock phosphates to your soil once every three to five years.

Potassium/potash (K): Why K? I don't know. Maybe because P was already taken! Why potash? I *really* don't know that one—maybe it needed an alias. Anyway, this confusingly synonymized nutrient essentially helps plants do *everything* better. It helps the flow of all the other nutrients throughout the plant, improves fruit quality, and helps the plant better resist stress. Two good stand-alone potassium sources:

- **Greensand** contains only a small amount of potassium but has a big effect, perhaps due to all the neat little micronutrients it also provides. Greensand also takes a while to break down, so you should add it to your soil the fall before you plant. Organic matter speeds its release, so some gardeners like to add greensand to their fall-built compost piles to supercharge the resulting "black gold"—a tactic I heartily recommend.

- **Sul-Po-Mag** is organic, despite its Madison Avenue name, and is *very* powerful stuff. It's also mined. A little goes a long way. Sul-Po-Mag contains magnesium (the "mag" part) as well, so you wouldn't ever want to use more than a pinch on tomatoes—it can interfere with calcium absorption, which the plants need and love more than the mag. Hmmm. Come to think of it, it's probably much better to get this nutrient from greensand—or from compost or grass clippings from clean lawns; both are rich in K.

And that's just the tiniest little tip of the NPK iceberg. Maybe we'll do a *You Bet Your Garden® Guide to Fertilizers!* book later on.

Greensand is a mined substance found in deposits formed in prehistoric oceans. (Yes! Dinosaur fertilizer!) Some of the biggest greensand mines are found in New Jersey. The secret behind the fabled Jersey tomato?

SOIL TESTING

This is fun to do, and many states offer a really inexpensive test through their County Extension Service—generally for under $10. Get in touch with your local extension office (do an Internet search for "County Cooperative Extension" and the name of your state), and they'll send you a kit to put your sample in (some nurseries sell the kits in spring as well). You fill it up (make sure the sample is a mixture of soil from all your big planting areas), send it in with a check, and you (and often your local extension agent as well) will receive the results. Most tests *don't* include your soil's nitrogen levels because they fluctuate a lot (some tests *will* reveal your soil's "organic matter content," which is similar), but all will list the levels of phosphorus and potassium, the pH of your soil (whether it's acidic or alkaline—you want it to be a little on the acidic side, like around 6.5 for most garden crops), and other cool stuff.

It's great to know what you have before you start adding things (especially lime), and it's fun—a horoscope for your dirt! Unfortunately, the Extension specialists and/or soil lab might recommend some really nasty chemicals to remedy any problems or imbalances. Just say no.

Note: For some reason, soil tests for most West Coast states are either unavailable or darned expensive compared to the rest of the country. If that's the case, check some out-of-state listings. Many state labs take out-of-state samples, a trick that could save you a good fifty bucks.

NUTRITION IN A NUTSHELL

Now, there are just a few things I want to be sure you take away from all this:

- *Compost* really is *the* best food—it supplies all the nutrients your plants need, in a form plants can use *easily*. Feed your plants with compost and "NPK" can be just three more magnetic letters cluttering up the outside of your fridge.

- If your plants are small, stunted, or otherwise don't seem to be growing, give them some nitrogen, but *don't* overdo it. And don't add nitrogen alone if your plants are already big and strong.

- If you want to add some *really* helpful stuff, enhance your garden soil with a little rock phosphate and greensand the season before. (Or add them to your fall compost piles and then feed your plants the finished compost.)

- If you buy fertilizer, make sure it's balanced. That *doesn't* mean equal numbers, like the dreaded 10-10-10. Remember, the ideal ratio is 3-1-2. If you can't find that, shoot for something close, like 4-2-3. And the 3-1-2 thing is a *ratio*, so a fertilizer that's 6-2-4 or 9-4-6 would also be close to perfect. But don't buy anything with numbers much higher than that—a nitrogen number over 11 or 12 is a good indication that the stuff ain't organic. And please, *don't* use chemical fertilizers; I don't care what your friends tell you—concentrated chemical salts are bad for plants and for the planet. And there's as good a chance they'll make your plants sick as you feed them.

- And don't overfeed, period! If you're using a packaged fertilizer, work the stuff into the soil when you put your plants in the ground, then mulch over it with a thin layer of compost. In a normal year in a normal climate, you should be set for the season. If you're a Nervous Nellie, give them a boost of compost tea or a dilute fish and seaweed fertilizer mid-season. If you're growing in a clime with a long, hot season, you can do two boosts. Maybe three if that season is long and the plants are really paying off big-time. But no more than that—and think compost, compost, compost!

WOOD CHIPS, SAWDUST, AND OTHER WOOD PRODUCTS

The ultimate tragedy is for me to hear from some poor schlep right *after* their helpful spouse has helpfully tilled a couple trash cans full of sawdust or wood chips into their garden to improve the soil. Which they have *not* done. No, instead they have created a killing field where no plants will grow for several years. Wood is the ultimate carbon source, and carbon seeks out nitrogen in an attempt to merge and decompose—and if you *mix a lot of carbon into your soil*, it'll suck the nitrogen right out of your good earth *until it finishes decomposing*. Which will be several years down the line. Many is the gardener who accidentally starved his plants to death because he had a big pile of wood chips burning a hole in his trowel right around planting time.

Same goes for wood ashes. Forget all the stuff you heard about Native Americans; those stories are about as historically reliable as an old "Lone Ranger" TV show script. Wood ashes are highly alkaline and will turn the average garden into a darned good imitation of Death Valley, where you don't see many tomatoes now, do you? Nope, just bleached cattle skulls.

Watering

Don't! Notice how I keep telling you *not* to do things? Most people do too many things. And watering too much is often one of them.

Now actually, this depends greatly on where you live. I garden in the land of traditionally wet seasons, where plants *rarely* need extra watering. Yes, some summers I have to water a lot. But some summers I have not needed to water even *once*. And *some* summers, I have wished desperately that I could somehow un-water my raised beds.

Anyway, it is easy to add water, but *really* difficult to remove water.

Now in some years, I have experienced a little taste of what it must be like to garden in Arizona. One season, it simply *did not* rain, and I learned that this can have a spiraling effect—the lack of rain made the air so dry it literally sucked any moisture I added right out of the soil, making a *theoretically* correct amount of added water turn out to be much less than the plants actually needed.

But I'm getting ahead of myself—let's start with the basics.

Bottom line: Keep track of your rainfall. An inexpensive rain gauge is a great investment. Here in the Northeast, we'll typically get one good soaking storm a week during the summer, and that's perfect. If a week

A rain gauge is essential to prevent overwatering. And underwatering. Just get one, OK?

MEASURING MOISTNESS

Let's say you've lost track of all rainfall. You're a character on one of those daytime soaps, and you've just emerged from a coma to find that your fiancée—who was told you were dead by a doctor with dyslexia—has accidentally married your long-lost separated-at-birth brother, who misled a mob boss into thinking your car was gold-plated under that ratty yellow paint. *And* you don't know when it last rained. Put a stick that will show wetness (like a paint stirrer) down into the soil a couple of inches. If you can see moistness, back off. *Don't water; the roots are still wet.* But, if you can jam it down in there to a depth of six inches (150 millimeters) or so (and if you can, congratulations! You've got great soil!) and still see only dry soil, go ahead and water.

Don't water because the *surface* of the soil is dry! The top inch (25 millimeters) or so of a garden can dry out *fast, but it doesn't count;* it's the moistness down at the root zone that counts.

And *never* water just because the leaves of a plant are wilting and it looks like it needs water. *Especially* if it's the middle of a hot and sunny day (that plant will probably perk right back up at sunset) and/or you've been pouring a bucketful on that poor baby every day for the past month, rain or shine. (That plant will *never* perk up again—because *over*watered plants look *exactly* like plants that need water.)

goes by without one, it's time to water—but not twenty minutes a night every night for a week; that promotes shallow root growth, and your plants will go out and vote for whoever promises them a tax cut. *And* you should *never* water in the *evening*, period!

When you need to provide supplemental water, you should try to do so like nature does/did/should have—a long, slow soaking that delivers an inch (25 millimeters) of water, once a week. I know, an inch doesn't sound like much, but think about those times it *poured* all night long, and then the local TV station's weather-guesser came on the next day and said: "Boy, that was a soaker, wasn't it? We got three-quarters of an inch!" An inch is a *lot*.

Now, the best time to water is in the morning, which can begin overnight if it takes a couple of hours for your system to deliver that inch—as long as you end the watering just as the morning sun begins to dry the plants off. *Don't* water in the evening and then stop *before* the sun rises; a plant that stays wet overnight will be an unhappy plant—*especially* a tomato plant. This is also true for lawns, lilacs, roses, and dogwoods—they're all drama queens about wet evenings. As am I, come to think of it.

If you sprinkle, and are uncertain how long it takes your particular sprinkler to deliver an inch (25 millimeters) of life-giving liquid, here's how to figure it out. Arrange a couple of rain gauges, tin cans, pint containers, etc., throughout the area to be watered, and then time how

Watering that wets the plants should only be done in the early morning, never in the evening.

long it takes them to fill up to one inch (25 millimeters). That's how long you want to water after that—but only, of course, *when* you have to water after that. Anyway, use a timer if the timing would require you to get up and turn it on at 3:30 in the morning and that makes you cranky.

Don't give your garden (or lawn, or whatever) a good soaking in the *evening* and then stop. It isn't good for *any* plant to sit around wet all night. A viable alternative (and one I have used) is to set that old alarm for 4 or 5 in the godforsaken, turn on the sprinkler, stagger back to bed, and then get up again and turn it off around 9 or 10 in the morning. Obviously, if you have (or get) a timer for your sprinkler, you can do this without having to get up.

And this really *is* what plants want—to be watered deeply, infrequently, and not sit out wet overnight.

I know some people just *love* to water their landscape every evening, because that's when the neighbors are out watching and they think it makes them look like Good And Decent People Who Are Paying Attention. But nighttime watering of any kind invites disease, and frequent short watering at any time of the day, night, or whatever leads to plants with shallow roots, which is as bad—possibly worse—than shallow people. And constant watering that never allows them feeble little roots to ever dry out completely will just plain *drown* the poor things. So you may look like a Good And Decent Person Who Is Paying Attention, but your plants will be dead.

Yes, plants really *do* want to have their tootsies dry out completely between waterings. Don't *you*?

In a typical summer, with typical rain, you shouldn't have to water much, if at all—especially if you've got a nice moisture-conserving mulch around the base of (but not touching) your plants to keep moisture in the soil. However, some gardens *will* dry out faster than others. These include:

- Gardens in full sun
- Gardens with un-mulched soil
- Gardens with sandy soil
- Gardens in a blisteringly hot climate
- Gardens in *any* climate during a blisteringly hot, biblically dry season

Pay attention to conditions and be prepared to deviate from these suggestions if the weather goes all blahooey.

A COUPLE OF APPLICATION OPTIONS

Yes, it is much better to water at the base of your tomato plants than to use a sprinkler, which wets the leaves. (You can't stop rain from doing that, but you can stop *you* from doing that.) If you want to leave a hose dripping away at the base of each of your plants for an hour or so, and then move it to the next one, ad infinitum, fine. You can even do this any time of the day or night. And, yes, this *is* better for the plants than a sprinkler. But a sprinkler set up high in the middle of a garden sure can take care of everything at once.

But the best way to water is with soaker hoses: specialized hoses that you lay on the surface of the soil and cover with mulch. The hoses either release small amounts of water through little pinholes or sweat the water out. They waste zero water, apply it at the slow rate plants love, *and* (unlike that sprinkler) only apply water where you want and do not water weeds.

Soaker hoses are especially worth looking into if you live in a traditionally dry clime and/or pay for your water and/or sometimes face water restrictions. (They can *see* the sprinkler spinning around; they *can't* see hoses sweating under your mulch!) I used soaker hoses for many years and was quite happy with the results. But now I've got a rotating sprinkler up on a big pole in the center of the garden for when I need it. I only run it early in the morning, it does a great job of wetting everything down, I don't care that it waters weeds because I pull and toss the weeds into the compost (green manure), and we can shoo the kids out into it to wash the stink off 'em during the summer. You can't go play in the soaker hose.

WATERING BASICS

An inch (25 millimeters) of water a week, preferably all at once, preferably delivered slowly and right at the root zone, and preferably *preferably* ending just as the sun rises in the early morning.

Really—that's it. And it's true for almost every plant: tomatoes, flowers, lawns, trees, those man-eating lily pads from the old Tarzan movies… An inch (25 millimeters) a week "from you or the sky," as the saying goes.

Soaker hoses, which release small amounts of water into the ground via little holes without wetting plant leaves, are a great way to water.

Pest Control and...
(Am I the only creature around here *not* eating my tomatoes?)

Dealing with Disease
(Can't we just take them to the hospital?)

. . . .

Well now, something has gone terribly wrong out there, hasn't it? And it's driven you to turn to this very special feature—two chapters in one.

Oh, come on—why *else* would you be reading this? There's no cutesy tomato names or fun tips about grinding up the hubcaps of 1975 Chevy Novas and placing a teaspoon of the resulting dust in each planting hole to supply the essential micronutrient molybdenum. (A deficiency of which, by the way, reveals itself in the form of yellow leaves on the plant. Unfortunately, as you are about to learn, so does just about every other nutrient deficiency, as well as three-quarters to ninety-eight percent of the diseases that strike tomatoes.)

Nope, you're here because you're in trouble. You've probably noticed that:

a)   something other than you is eating your tomatoes; or

b)   your plants look like you did last flu season, stretched out on the couch in the middle of the afternoon, watching talk shows.

The good news:

Pest problems on tomatoes are surprisingly rare and, when they do occur, are almost always pretty easy to deal with—organically, of course!

The other news:

Disease problems on tomatoes are about as rare as someone emailing you to say that you just won a Nigerian lottery you're pretty sure you never entered.

Hey! Let's do those pests first, shall we?

Beefsteak

Beefsteak is one of those variety names that has escaped its singularity and is often used now to describe a type of tomato. You'll find seeds and plants simply labeled "Beefsteak," but there are probably dozens of adjectival versions out there as well. I like this meaty **Porterhouse Beefsteak** example. No matter the name, Beefsteaks should all be big, tasty, "beefy" tomatoes.

Photo by Xfigpower.

The tomato hornworm might look like a harmless caterpillar, but it can quickly destroy your tomato crop.

Photo by Fritz Geller-Grimm.

Although the Colorado potato beetle is primarily known as a potato plant pest, it can also be a major problem for tomato gardeners.

Tomato Pests

Probably the best-known tomato pest, the *tomato hornworm* (which looks a lot like the tobacco hornworm, a similar caterpillar that will also eat your plants to the ground) is a *big* green caterpillar (one of the biggest!). It eats the foliage of your plants and, despite defoliating a surprising amount of plant matter, is almost impossible to see because it is the *exact* same color as the leaves being eaten. In fact, most people who *do* notice a hornworm actually either first notice the big black piles of "frass" (a twenty-dollar word for bug poop) all over their plants, the defoliated status of the plants themselves, or they catch a glimpse of the neat-looking white "spines" running down the caterpillar's back, which make it look a little like a stegosaurus, but much easier to squish.

If you see those white things, guess what? Pest problem solved! And don't squish!

Those spines are *not* standard equipment on your basic hornworm. What looks a lot like little grains of white rice are actually the cocoons of a tiny beneficial wasp that preys on pest caterpillars.

There are millions of different species of such mini-wasps flying around out there, all the size of a period at the end of a sentence. All are too small to sting us, but they just *love* to lay their eggs in or on caterpillars. When the eggs hatch…that's right—bursting out of your garden pests just like in the movie *Alien*!

If you see an *un*adorned hornworm, just squish it—or try and raise it to moth stage as described in the sidebar on page 93. If you see one with the white "rice" on its back, however, leave it in the garden. Soon, a fresh squadron of caterpillar-parasitizing mini-wasps will emerge from their cocoons to do garden pest control for you.

This, by the way, is Reason #162 for not using chemical pesticides in your garden. Today's pests mostly just shrug the poisons off (thank you, Mr. Darwin!), but when beneficial bugs get sprayed, they fold up fast.

Colorado potato beetles. This beetle is included here because a *huge* number of gardeners, garden writers, county extension agents, and others have told me lurid tales of their tomato plants being eaten to the ground by these ravenous bugs. The larval (baby) form are kind of humpbacked, softish, the consistency of snot, and have round black spots on their side panels. The adults look like—and are—rogue ladybugs (technically ladybird beetles; they're not true bugs), of which there are two *bad* family members (the other one's busy decimating your string beans). Adult CPBs have hard shell cases covering a set of wings

RAISE YOUR OWN HORNWORM

As a household science project, try raising a hornworm to cocoon stage and beyond in captivity. (The *enormous* hornworm caterpillar, its *really* scary larvae (big, segmented, big, brown, big, and wiggly), and the resulting sphinx moth are all huge and impressive. Big, too. Just pot up an infested plant (or put a load of cut tomato branches and a hornworm [non-parasitized: no little white spines on its back] on a big pot of soil), cover it all with netting, and put it on a porch or in the basement. When you can't find the caterpillar anymore, remove the netting. If this *is* for a science project, wait a couple weeks and then dig out the ginormous, wriggling, brown, segmented larvae pupating in the soil. Take a picture and put it back in the pot and cover it with some more dirt. In a month or so, you'll be attacked by a giant Mothra-like creature known as the sphinx moth. A huge beast. Take more pictures. Capture the monster and take it to school. On a leash.

Wasn't that fun? A lot more fun than letting the wormy weasel eat your plants to the ground outside…

(as do all beetles), black stripes, and look a *lot* like ladybugs. Both stages are around half an inch (15 millimeters) long, orange-ish yellow, and do a *lot* of damage.

(I'm actually feeling a little sad and left out here. I mean, I've never had any potato bugs on my tomatoes. Now, my life has not exactly been pest- and problem-free, you know? But it's like I'm missing one baseball card out of a complete set… Garden Pests! Collect 'em! Trade 'em! Stick 'em in the spokes of your bike so they make noise!)

Your best CPB control option is a specific form of the organic insecticide known as *Bt*. A number of different varieties of *Bt* (which stands for *Bacillus thuringiensis*) are used in organic pest control; all are naturally occurring living organisms found in soils throughout the world. Lots of different strains of *Bt* have been discovered, but only a few are being used, and all of those are used to kill pest insects—and only one specific type of pest insect per *Bt*. The mode of action is perfect: You spray a solution of *Bt* onto a plant and then, when the target pest nibbles away at the plant, the *Bt* gets into the pest's stomach and shuts it down. So not only does the pest eventually die, it stops eating your stuff right away. The *Bt* can't harm anything other than its specific type of target pest, and it can't harm *anything* that doesn't actually eat the leaves of a *Bt*-sprayed plant. And each variety of *Bt* is *so* specific that it wouldn't even harm a different type of pest eating the same leaves. It won't harm you, your pets, your birds, your toads…

The oldest and best-known form of *Bt* (the *Bacillus thuringiensis kurstaki* strain, or BTK) is used to kill caterpillar pests. In fact, it's what you'd spray on your plants to control hornworms if those poor puppies

BEETLES REUNION

REMEMBER WHEN WE PLAYED MIKE'S GARDEN? WHAT A PERFORMANCE!

If the dreaded CPB does come a-calling on your German Johnsons, you really should do something about it. These thugs have decimated my potato plants in the past, so I know the damage they can do.

weren't so pitifully vulnerable to teeny-tiny wasp attacks already. For potato beetles, you want the variety *tenebrionis,* which is sold under the brand names Colorado Potato Beetle Beater and Novodor. The three-letter abbreviation for this specific *Bt* is BTT. (This *Bt*'s original surname was San Diego, but apparently that was too easy to remember and spell. So if you see a reference to *Bt* San Diego, it's the same stuff.)

Mix up a batch as directed and spray it on the leaves of your tomato plants (do any potatoes in your garden as well). The pests will die soon after eating the sprayed leaves.

Other control options: Hand-pick and drop the offenders into a jar of soapy water, or vacuum the adults off! Works great—just be sure you're plugged into a ground-fault outlet or use a rechargeable vac.

If, like me, you must garden in a sometimes shady spot, you'll probably also have to deal with *slugs*. I hate slugs.

If you see big whopping holes in your fruit (green or ripe), slugs have probably slimed their way up there and are dining on *your* tomatoes late in the evening while you sleep. They must be killed. Dead.

You can make *sure* it's slugs by going out into the garden—especially when it's still wet from a recent rain—late some evening (after 10 p.m.) with a flashlight, a spray bottle loaded with a half-and-half mixture of white vinegar and water, and a shaker filled with salt. If slugs *are* nibbling your plants, you'll see 'em. Spray some with the vinegar. See how they shrivel up!

You can also salt them. This is lots of fun. Don't salt them like French fries, though—just one little crystal on each of their slimy little selves is all it takes. You may not notice anything bad happening to them right away, but by morning your salted slugs will have become little blobs of orange goop. Despite the immense satisfaction this may give you, resist the urge to do this often, because you don't want to be salting your garden. Think of it as an occasional reward for staying up late.

Buy this slug a beer at sundown before he (she? it?) does more damage.

OK—now, repulsed by the knowledge that this seething mass of living snot is out there devouring your precious garden plants every evening, you are now ready to wage war against these miserable mollusks. To wit:

- Lay flat wooden boards down between your raised beds or alongside your plants. The slugs, like vampires, will crawl under the boards when the sun rises. You go out early in the morning, lift the boards, and use a long, flat piece of metal or wood to scrape the massed slugs thereon into a bucket with an inch (25 millimeters) of soapy water in the bottom.

- Leave out beer traps in which they will drown overnight. Now, if you're thinking "Oh yeah—somebody told me about that; they said to use stale beer," think again. Slugs like stale beer about as much as I do. Collect some old margarine tubs, fill them up with *fresh* beer (the yeastier the better), and set them with the rims an inch or two (25 to 50 millimeters) above the soil surface around plants that have been attacked. Do this at *sunset* so the heat of the day doesn't flatten the brew. In the morning, your traps will be filled with drowned, drunken slugs. Empty your catch (that nasty mess will now *repel* potential new victims), refill at sunset (so the beer doesn't lose flavor during the day), and repeat. Three words of advice if you like the beer method of slug control: cheapest brand available.

- Surround your plants with copper barriers. Slugs can't touch copper (it's like vampires and garlic).

- Surround your plants with crushed-up eggshells. Slugs can't slither over their pointy-sharp edges.

- Buy a bag of diatomaceous earth (DE) and use it to make mystic circles around your plants. DE looks like flour but is actually the pulverized remains of prehistoric ocean-dwelling creatures called diatoms. Very cool. It feels soft to us, but on a microscopic level is jagged and sharp and will pierce the slugs' slippery little bodies. Wear a mask so you won't breathe the dust (or *any* dusty garden stuff).

No matter how much you're tempted, don't drop any slugs you find in your garden into gasoline, kerosene, or some other recommended-by-a-complete-idiot nonsense. It isn't necessary—soapy water works great; and just what were you going to do with this highly polluting, federally-illegal-in-this-form (and explosive) liquid afterward, Mr. or Mrs. Environmental-Criminal-To-Be?

Crushed eggshells basically act like razor wire for slugs: the sharp edges prevent them from slithering onto your tomatoes.

Eventually you'll figure out that you're buying beer for creatures eating your garden to the ground. (And if you choose to continue anyway, two words: "cheap beer." Treat those slugs to the best case a five-spot can buy.

Evil Squirrels and Dastardly Deer can be shameless tomato thieves.

Occasionally I hear from people whose tomatoes are being eaten by *squirrels*. Well, if it's any consolation, the squirrels might not really be all that interested in your tomatoes. They're either:

a) Thirsty. In a dry season, squirrels will get water wherever they can, and your tomatoes are full of it. Leave some water out for them to drink, and just maybe they'll leave your love apples alone; or

b) looking for amusement. Squirrels are evil, easily amused, evil, and love the performance you put on whenever they get near your tomatoes. The solution is easy: move. To another state. Not an adjoining one, either. *Those* squirrels already heard about you.

Actually, a motion-activated sprinkler (one of the most popular is The Scarecrow) works well against both squirrels and deer. You set it up, aim it toward the plants you wish to protect, and it throws a couple cups of cold water at anything that breaks the motion-detecting beam. (Makes cats levitate; lots of fun!) Yes, you're sure to get wet too, but that's a small price to pay for unmolested love apples.

Deer will also eat tomatoes. And everything else. If you don't have a garden, they'll eat your car. Get a motion-activated sprinkler. Or two.

Groundhogs will eat lots of your tomatoes. The surest way to keep them out is with a fence. But it *has* to be buried at least one-and-a-half feet (450 millimeters) deep in the ground, preferably more (they dig for a living), you have to stake the regular straight-up part of the fence really well (they can pull *real* hard), *and* you need to *not* stake the very top foot (300 millimeters) but to bend it outward, unsupported, like a baffle. Because they also climb. Really, really well. *But,* when they reach that outward-facing baffle, their fat and furry rear ends will get plopped back down on the ground—outside your garden.

Fun to watch! Six-foot-tall fence: two feet buried, three feet staked, top foot baffled out. Guaranteed. (That's a 2-meter fence with 600 millimeters buried, 900 millimeters staked, and 300 millimeters baffled out for you Metrics.)

Or get outdoor cats. *Tough* outdoor cats; no sissy cat pretenders. Barn cats. Biker cats. Cats with tats! Or a Jack Russell terrier.

You might also encounter problems with birds. They're probably more legitimately thirsty than the evil squirrels. The solution: a birdbath. If they don't stop attacking your tomatoes after you provide the water they *should* be wanting, get mean. Hang big red round Christmas tree balls on your plants. Very festive, but tough on the old beak.

That's about it. Yeah, there's also things like tomato fruitworms and such (the cure for which, by the way, is to spray BTK on your plants), but they're not all that common. A more likely cause of loss at this point is your neighbor slipping into the garden late at night to filch some ripe ones. (Solution: motion-activated sprinkler.)

Tomato Diseases

Two soil-borne wilts are very common tomato problems: *verticillium* and *fusarium wilt*. These two fungal diseases are difficult to tell apart. Both begin with a yellowing and wilting of the lower leaves of your plant, which is real helpful, because yellow leaves are *also* a sign of:

- nitrogen deficiency
- iron deficiency
- zinc deficiency
- potassium deficiency
- calcium deficiency
- aphids
- tobacco mosaic virus
- root-knot nematodes
- being too close to a black walnut tree
- the heartbreak of psoriasis

If you've fed your plants lots of nice compost (or a good, balanced organic fertilizer) and put some crushed-up eggshells into the planting hole like I already told you to, yellow leaves are probably *not* a sign of a hunger problem. Black walnut trees nearby? You're outta luck. Buy a new house or plant in big containers next year. You can't grow tomatoes within a hundred feet (30 meters) of a black walnut any more than Superman can play catch with Kryptonite.

But if your tomatoes are simply planted where other tomatoes have grown in previous years, it could well just be one of the wilts. Most likely *verticillium* if you grow in a cooler clime (like me), or *fusarium* for you warm-clime gardeners. Don't worry *too* much—if you haven't planted tomatoes in that same spot for several years running, most plants will still provide you a good amount of fruit. Indeterminate plants—especially big rangy heirlooms—can sometimes "outrun" the

Promptly pull off discolored leaves so the neighbors think your plants are healthier than theirs.

Don't plant tomatoes anywhere near the dripline of a black walnut tree; the roots contain a naturally occurring compound called juglone that kills tomatoes dead.

disease, with their aggressive new growth appearing faster than the old stuff can yellow up. Unfortunately, determinate plants don't run nearly as fast and will be knocked to the ground. In either case, the disease does not affect the actual fruit, and any *tomatoes* the plants produce are safe to eat.

But mark the areas where such plants are growing (maybe you can buy a pack of little Jolly Roger pirate flags at the Dollar Store!), and don't plant tomatoes in those spots the next two seasons. *And* consider growing varieties known to resist these diseases the next time out. Such tomatoes will have the letters *V* and *F* after their variety name on seed packets and in catalog descriptions. Most resistant varieties these days sport four letters—VFNT—meaning that they also resist root-knot nematodes (a serious problem down South, but a non-issue in the North) and tobacco mosaic virus.

No matter what, pull off any discolored leaves as soon as they appear. It'll slow the progression of the disease, open up the base of the plant to improved airflow, and—most important—make it look like your plants are doing better than they actually are.

Early blight and *late blight* are fungal pests that can really lay low your love apples (and your potatoes, too). The first signs of true blight are target-like spots on the lower leaves. These dark spots usually spread and run together. You might also see dark spots on the stems and (shudder) on the stem ends of the bee-yoo-tee-ful tomatoes themselves. If spots appear *on* your *fruit*, that plant is toast. Pull it up, throw it in the trash, and hope it didn't infect your other plants. These bad guys hang out in debris in your garden, just waiting to infect next year's plants. So don't leave old tomato plants in the garden over winter, don't plant in the same spot, and remove all old mulches at the beginning of every season.

There are a bazillion other diseases that can affect tomatoes—the further south (and the more humid) your growing location, the more diseases there are to attack your patch. (But you'll also have a longer season than us cool-climers, and thus more of a replanting option when and if the Black Plague strikes—so don't complain.)

And don't be surprised if one or two plants rot away on you while the others look fine, especially in a wet year. One plant coming down with the tomato flu does not necessarily mean it's going to spread through your garden like it's a day care center.

Early blight is more likely to infect stressed plants. Get out there and teach them some relaxation techniques before it's too late!

Compost Cream

As with us humans, it is easier to *prevent* tomato diseases than to cure them after they show up. So do the things I told you to do in the planting section, and you either won't have the problem to begin with or your troubles will be little ones.

Specifically:

- Keep all parts of the plants off the ground.
- Make sure there's good air circulation around each plant.
- Plant them where they get the earliest possible morning sun.
- Keep an inch or two (25 to 50 millimeters) of fresh compost on the soil around your plants.
- Don't plant tomatoes in the same spot again for a few years.
- Light a candle to the blessed tomato deity of your choice.

If disease *does* show up:

- Remove any diseased leaves, stems, or even whole branches *immediately*. This slows down the spread of disease. Throw them in the trash. Do not compost or bury them. If a whole plant looks *really* bad, pull it up and trash it. Really—it's Typhoid Mary in tomato drag.
- Remove all the old mulch from under and around the affected plant and replace it with an inch or two (25 to 50 millimeters) of nice, fresh compost. This will eliminate any disease spores lurking on the ground, create a fresh layer of disease-munching microorganisms, and confuse the Dickens out of any slugs that were hiding down there.
- If your plants are really crowded and some of the plants in that crowd are all yellowed up while others are fine, get the sad-looking ones outta there. Again, into the trash, *not* the compost!
- Do anything you can to improve airflow to the garden proper and especially to your languishing love apples. Yes, this may involve moving or simply removing some other plants. Wet year? *Gotta* do it.
- Spray the secret formula(s) of your choice.

Secret Formulas!

Although far from secret, these formulas *can* be very effective at preventing or fighting tomato disease difficulties.

Preventing: If you garden in a warm wet clime, have had troubles with tomato disease in previous seasons, are forced to plant where tomatoes have grown before, or are just nervous as all get out about such things, you can use any of the following formulas as a preventive. None of them will harm your plants, and the two compost tea ones will actually give 'em a nice little snack as well as some disease protection. You can spray any of these things as often as every two weeks—moving up to every week if the leaves of your plants begin to look a little suspicious.

Fighting: Get rid of *all* diseased leaves on the plant first. Don't spray discolored leaves hoping that somehow the Laws of Reality have suddenly lurched in your favor. Spray the entire plant really, really well, especially the undersides of the leaves—get in there and rub them with your fingers if you can. Then replace the mulch underneath, but *after* you spray, because you may otherwise wash some undead disease spores down there. Start out with weekly sprays, and then increase or decrease the frequency, depending on the response, the weather, and your patience for this sort of thing.

#1: "THE CORNELL FORMULA" BAKING SODA AND OIL SPRAY—A NATURAL PLANT FUNGICIDE

Developed at Cornell University, this baking soda–based remedy is a great spray-on plant disease preventer/fighter. It's as good as any chemical fungicide you can buy. To use this formula, get a sprayer—anything from a handheld one-gallon (four-liter) job to one of those really cool big-boy backpack styles. Just make sure it's never been used to spray herbicides, or it's bye-bye Brandywines.

The Recipe:

In one gallon (four liters) of water, mix:

- ☑ 1 tablespoon baking soda
- ☑ 1 tablespoon oil (see note below)
- ☑ 1 or 2 drops dishwashing liquid

Shake well and then spray on the plant you wish to protect and/or rescue; keep shaking the sprayer regularly while you're working.

Don't spray under direct sun in the heat of the day. Early morning is best.

Note: The ideal oil to use here is horticultural oil, known to many folks generically as dormant oil, a term that actually refers to the old, original version—a very heavy petroleum-based product that is *only* safe to use on big woody plants in the dead of winter (the dormant period). For *this* recipe, you want to use one of the newer lightweight horticultural oils (sometimes called all season oils or summer sprays), available at most nurseries and garden centers. In a pinch, you can use regular vegetable oil from the kitchen, but a real hort oil will work better. And *no*, you duct-tape gardeners, you *can't* be a cowboy and use motor oil or WD-40 or any other such foolish thing.

#2: BASIC COMPOST TEA

Many folks tell me they've postponed, put off, and even successfully battled plant diseases head-on by spraying regular old compost tea (ROCT) on their plants. And since it takes two weeks to make the superior-at-disease-fighting fermented version (FCT; described next), you might as well give it a try while your heavy artillery is brewing.

Make up a batch of compost tea like I told you to back on page 79. Strain the diluted "tea" through some cheesecloth (so it doesn't clog up your sprayer), then pour it into a sprayer

Big Beef is an early hybrid beefsteak (duh!) type variety prized for its size, productivity, and old-time tomato flavor.

tank and spray it on the plant's leaves the very first thing in the morning, when the plant is most receptive to this kind of thing. Make sure you get at the undersides of the leaves; hold the sprayer low and shoot upward. *Don't* spray in the heat of the day or in the evening.

#3: FERMENTED COMPOST TEA

The killer. The winnah. The strongest plant disease fighter/preventer known to man or woman. Tackles tomato diseases so hard it makes 'em cry. Defeats black spot on roses. Swear to God. This baby can't be beat.

To create fermented compost tea (FCT), first make compost tea. Pour an undiluted (strong coffee) batch into a big bucket and let it sit in a shady spot for two weeks. Cover the top of the container with window screening to keep out breeding mosquitoes, or you'll get a nasty surprise when you jiggle it the first time. Filthy-looking scum will form on top of the liquid. This is good. Skim off the scum and toss it back onto your compost pile. Then, *very* carefully and slowly, pour off some of the liquid that was underneath said scum through a fine strainer and into a sprayer. Slow down! There's a big batch of solids in the bottom of the bucket that you want to leave there, or you'll clog up your strainer. Toss those solids back onto the compost pile, too.

Use FCT early in the season before the plants are fruiting, applying it as you would the Cornell formula. The advantage of FCT over baking-soda-and-oil spray? The compost tea is *alive* with millions of tiny organisms that eat disease organisms, so you're spraying an army of Pac-Man-like soldiers that will literally eat diseases to death right on your plants. Very exciting; just be sure to wash up thoroughly after you've applied FCT to make sure you don't expose yourself to any errant bacteria.

Chapter 8

The Harvest and Beyond

(Aren't they supposed to stop being green at some point?)

(So this one here cost me about forty bucks, right?)

(Can the kids use the green ones to play Mr. Tomato Head?)

Tomatoes, especially the most flavorful heirloom varieties, are unique among the things we eat in that we experience much of their flavor through the *nose* rather than the taste buds. Really. Bite into a big pink Brandywine, and much of its great flavor is transmitted to your tomato-loving brain through your *olfactory* senses.

That's because much of a tomato's fine flavor is contained in volatile aromatic compounds produced in the ripening fruit.

(By the way, the answers to the questions above are: it depends, probably, and absolutely!)

Heirloom

Heirloom tomatoes such as these, prized for their diverse colors and shapes, only exist because dedicated gardeners and farmers saved the seeds from their best fruit after the variety was no longer offered commercially, grew them out the following year, saved the seeds from the best of that crop, planted them the following season, ad infinitum. Without that dedication, many of these treasured tomatoes would have been lost to the mists of time.

Helpful Harvest Hints

Because these *are* volatile aromatic compounds, a ripe tomato left sitting out in the sun will begin to lose flavor—quickly. Rapidly, even. If you've always let your tomatoes get dead ripe on the vine before picking, you're in for a treat—start bringing them in a little sooner and you'll notice a tremendous surge in flavor.

So:

- Don't let ripe tomatoes sit on the vine; harvest them promptly.
- Don't be shy about bringing them in a little early. Once it's started to color up, any tomato will finish ripening just fine on its own. I personally bring my tomatoes in when they're about half colored up—they're no longer getting nutrition or anything important from the vine, it's really just support at this point. Letting them finish ripening indoors gives me optimum flavor *and* protects the ripe and tempting fruit from last-minute pest attacks (stink bugs and squirrels *especially* love to mount late-in-the-game assaults).
- And when you *do* bring your not-quite-ripe ones (or end-of-season green tomatoes) indoors, do not put them on a sunny windowsill! That's what you just saved them from. Only tomato *leaves* can process sunlight. The tomatoes themselves—*any* fruit actually—are just hanging around letting the leaves collect energy for their benefit. Direct sun does *not* benefit fruit, and in some circumstances can actually harm it (especially via a condition called sunscald).

The above is one reason I don't promote the "pruning" or "suckering" of tomato plants. Do you really think you can give them more energy by ripping off some of their solar panels?

GREEN TOMATOES

Green tomatoes are fun to eat!
Green tomatoes are really neat!
Hoooray! For green tomatoes!

> Do not ever, under any circumstances, put a tomato in the refrigerator. You think heat dissipates those compounds? Well, cold'll finish 'em off. Don't do it.

If temps below 40°F (4.4°C) are coming, pull off all your green tomatoes; mature ones will ripen up on a kitchen counter indoors. Or make fried green tomatoes!

At the end of the season you can either waste more hours of your life trying to protect your still-green tomatoes from frost by covering the plants with large sheets of plastic every night and then *promptly* removing those covers every morning (and we do mean *promptly*— otherwise your tomatoes will cook when the sun heats up that plastic like vinyl car seats in the summertime)…

…or you can (sound of angelic chorus rising majestically): *Just. Be. Done!*

Yes, be done and watch the World Series. Once the sun begins to set depressingly early and the nighttime temps become noticeably colder, your tomatoes are pretty much going to go into suspended animation, and twenty years of experience has shown me you can easily expend around an eight-hour day's worth of work for every green tomato you actually coax a little more toward ripeness.

So when frost is called for, call the game. Strip all your green tomatoes off and bring 'em inside.

OK. OK. If one or two plants are loaded with medium-sized fruit, you think it might *not* actually frost (and you can smell the long warm Indian summer that is certain to follow), *and* your adventure tank has not been filled up by all the excitement you had so far over the summer, sure—go ahead and bundle those babies up. But don't use plastic; plastic is a sucker bet. Instead, buy floating row covers. These spun polyethylene blankets are sold in rolls under many brand names, the best known being Reemay.

Big advantage: You don't have to go out and do a split in your cold wet garden every morning as you struggle to remove your floating row covers. They breathe, so you can leave them on day *and* night. They'll provide a nice amount of frost protection at night and physically deter any late-season pests during the day. And when you *finally* do give up on your tomatoes, you can use the covers to stretch your salad green season an extra month or so. When salad time is finally over, remove the covers, hang them up until they're nice and dry, brush the dirt off them, roll them up, and save them—with a little care, they should last for quite a few years.

SPECIAL TIP

If it's September, pick flowers! When you know that frost is coming in a couple of weeks, ruthlessly pull off any new flowers that appear on your tomato plants. No, you aren't mad at them—your flower pulling will get the plant to devote more energy to ripening up the fruit that has already formed. And those flowers didn't have a prayer of having enough time to become full-sized tomatoes.

No, these little **Black Pearl** beauties don't look all that black (yet), but gaze closer and you'll see the streaks showing the beginning of their transition to a final, dusky color. It's lots of fun to watch the progression of black tomatoes in the garden, and as you can see here, black varieties come in all sizes, from giant beefsteak types to these soon-to-be-dusky little cuties. Whatever their size, all black tomatoes tend to have a naturally smoky flavor.

And be assured that any full-sized, fully grown green tomatoes (ones that were *just* getting ready to ripen) and tomatoes at the breaker stage (showing those hopeful blushes of color) *will* ripen up indoors. Just leave them out in the open—in a single layer—and use them as they ripen. Check them frequently—*especially* if they're piled up—for bad ones. A rotting tomato often looks sound at first glance, but closer inspection reveals that it's leaking nasty fluid and has an odor that could repel a skunk. That's why I sit my greenies out in long, low cardboard box bottoms that hold only one layer of tomatoes (no stacking!) and check 'em all every day.

Ripening on command. Well, pretty much on command. When all you have is green tomatoes and you really want some red (or black, or purple, or…) back in your life, you can push a green tomato toward ripeness more quickly by putting it (or a bunch of its) into a paper bag with a ripe banana, an apple, or a ripe tomato.

Those ripe fruits naturally give off ethylene gas, a manufactured version of which is used to gas-ripen commercial tomatoes, which are almost always picked green and hard for easy transport. Your "natural gassing" will speed up the ripening process greatly. Roll the bag lightly closed—but don't seal it shut or anything, and *don't* use plastic (the paper bag can "breathe," which is essential here). Make sure you check it *every* day.

Mr. Tomato Head. More greenies than you can possibly use? Give a couple of big *hard* ones to the kids, who can then play with Mr. Tomato Head from Outer Space! ('Cause he's *green*, see?)

My Super-Fast Saucing Tip!

Most of my tomatoes are grown to be put up. This involves sealing sauce and paste in Mason jars.

To get a really rich flavor, I sauce lots of different kinds of tomatoes together—big heirlooms like Georgia Streak, Brandywine, Mortgage Lifter, and Black Krim; traditional pasters like Roma and Bellstar; and less-traditional ones like Amish Paste and such.

MRS McGRATH'S FALL CLOSET

"Canning" up sauce in Mason jars allows you to enjoy your harvest through the winter. Unless your plants died.

The big, juicy ones add *lots* of flavor (and sometimes weird colors) to the finished product, but can make the process take a lot longer because of the extra non-meaty liquid they bring into the mix. So over the years, I've developed a method that produces lots of nice thick sauce *quickly*—which is not only important in time saved, but also helps preserve the vitamins and other heat-sensitive nutrients in the finished sauce. Here's the technique, along with my basic sauce-making recipe, so you can continue to enjoy your tomato harvest right up until you get fresh ones again the following season.

1) Collect all your nice ripe tomatoes, wash them well, and cut them right down the center so you can easily carve out the stem part. If a tomato has a few imperfections or bug holes, cut them away completely as well. Same with mottled skins—peel them off. If in doubt about a tomato's wholesomeness, don't use it.

2) Other people always remove the skins; I *don't* remove any skins that are perfect in texture. I figure it's nice solid tomato stuff and contains nutrients not found in other parts of the fruit. And the Vitamix food processor I use is so powerful they just disappear into the blend.

3) For years, people tried to convince me to remove the seeds. I did *not*, figuring they were doing a nice little Scrubbing Bubbles thing as they passed through us. But I found over the years that re-cooked sauces did seem to get a little bitter sometimes, which most sources blame on the seeds. So recently, I started scooping out and tossing the seeds and their scary gelatinous coating and, lo and behold, the finished sauce *is* sweeter. And there's a lot less liquid to deal with at cooking time. So I have come around on the seed thing since the last edition of this book (although I'm not compulsive about getting every last one, just most of them). Still keep the skins though.

Cut your tomatoes down the center (top) to make stem and seed removal easy, then pop those babies into a blender (bottom) with garlic and basil.

4) Chop your tomatoes up in batches and mostly fill up a blender or food processor with each chopped batch. But before you go whizzing, add one or more of the following to each batch:

- Onions: I add two or three big ones to each two-gallon (eight-liter) pot of sauce
- Garlic: I add four or five bulbs—not cloves, bulbs—to each pot.
- Herbs: Basil, oregano, whatever you like, whatever you got, as much as you got. (Warning: Thai basil = purple sauce!)

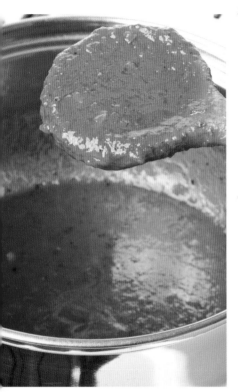

Beautiful! This photo even smells good!

5) Optional: Hoisin sauce. I will *not* add sugar or salt to my sauce (because *my* tomatoes *already* taste good). But a little extra sweetness is sometimes nice, and so when I feel like it, I add a couple glugs of this fabulous Chinese seasoning sauce to the mix—hoisin is kind of like plum sauce, but more complex. It used to be available only in Chinese grocery stores (or in those little containers provided for you to use on the inside of the pancake when you get take out and have to build your own Moo Shu chicken or pork thingies), but now I often see it in bottles and jars in American supermarkets.

6) Chop your seasoning things up finely, toss a batch into the blender/mixer with your chopped-up tomatoes, add a glug or two of hoisin sauce if you're walking that side of the street, and whiz everything up together (this mixes the seasonings in better than you could possibly achieve otherwise). Pour the resulting glop into a big stainless steel (not aluminum!) stockpot. And then repeat: another batch of tomatoes with seasonings, whizz, plop; then another, whizz, plop. Once you got a couple inches (75 to 100 millimeters or so) of stuff in the pot, turn the heat on to simmer.

7) When everything's in the pot and you can whiz and plop no more, give it about twenty minutes to heat up. In the meantime, get your canning stuff together: glass jars and rims that have just been washed and are still nice and hot from the dishwasher, a pot of water to heat your lids, a big "canning pot" three-quarters full of water in which to do the actual canning, etc. Add some freshly ground black pepper to the pot, and stir well.

8) Now the cool time-saving part. You'll notice that the really liquid, watery stuff is all rising to the top of the cooking pot. So get another, slightly smaller stainless steel pot and a strainer. Using a big-handled cup, keep skimming the liquid stuff off the top of your main pot and pour it through the strainer into the smaller pot. Anything that gets stuck in the strainer gets plopped back into the sauce pot. Keep going, stirring the rapidly thickening sauce as you do. When the liquid is mostly gone, begin using the stuff that gets trapped in the strainer to fill your first run of jars—a nice batch of wonderfully thick sauce.

9) You can simply jar up the liquid stuff in the secondary pot separately when you have all the real sauce done and processed,

or you can add another level of coolness. That secondary liquid will *also* separate, with a light tomato juice rising to the surface and lots of pasty-type solids dropping to the bottom. If you have a big, sparkling-clean glass jar, pour your "juice" into it and wait five or ten minutes—you'll see a clear line of demarcation. Using a clean turkey baster, suck the lighter-colored thin stuff off the top. I put this tomato juice into quart-size (liter) glass jars in the fridge and use it to make tomato soup or in place of some of the cooking water when I make soup stock.

10) Jar up the darker-colored thick stuff that settled down low in your secondary pot as your last canning run. You can use this "almost tomato paste" to make ridiculously rich tomato soups or, with a little cooking down, a wonderful naturally smooth sauce.

11) Follow the canning directions that came with your canning jars and lids *exactly*. Tomatoes are the easiest foods to can—their high acid content makes them one of the only foods you can put up safely without a pressure cooker. But still, be careful—make *sure* the jars are *really* sterilized (I always time a dishwasher run so the jars are clean and hot when the sauce is ready), that the lids are brand new and warmed up (you can re-use rims, but not lids), and that everything you use is good and clean. Wipe the tops of the jars with a clean, dry paper towel before you put the lids on, and all that stuff. I generally cook my pints of sauce and paste for twenty to thirty minutes in the canner. Oh—make sure you have a "jar lifter" tool (sold wherever they have canning supplies) at the ready, so you can safely lift the scalding hot jars out of the boiling water without giving yourself second degree burns, or even worse—dropping a jar!

12) Enjoy, brag, be proud!

And that's it! Thanks, have fun, and I'll see you in the next book.

Mike McGrath

Cool-Stuff Sources

Looking for rare, hard-to-find varieties? Need some specialized tool or organic elixir that your local garden center doesn't carry? Here are some mail-order suppliers who can help you along on your path to homegrown tomato nirvana.

Seeds

BOUNTIFUL GARDENS
18001 Shafer Ranch Road
Willits, CA 95490
Phone: (707) 459-6410
www.bountifulgardens.org

W. ATLEE BURPEE
300 Park Avenue
Warminster, PA 18974
Phone: (800) 888-1447
www.burpee.com

THE COOK'S GARDEN
P.O. Box C5030
Warminster, PA 18974
Phone: (800) 457-9703
www.cooksgarden.com

FEDCO SEEDS
P.O. Box 520
Waterville, ME 04903
Phone: (207) 873-7333
www.fedcoseeds.com

GURNEY'S SEED & NURSERY CO.
P.O. Box 4178
Greendale, IN 47025
Phone: (513) 354-1491
www.gurneys.com

HEIRLOOM SEED PROJECT
Landis Valley Museum
2451 Kissel Hill Road
Lancaster, PA 17601
Phone: (717) 569-0401
www.landisvalleymuseum.org
/seeds.php

HENRY FIELD'S SEED & NURSERY CO.
P.O. Box 397
Aurora, IN 47001
Phone: (513) 354-1495
www.henryfields.com

J. L. HUDSON, SEEDSMAN
P.O. Box 337
La Honda, CA 94020
No phone (a source of pride for these wonderful wackos)
www.jlhudsonseeds.net

JOHNNY'S SELECTED SEEDS

955 Benton Avenue
Winslow, ME 04901
Phone: (877) 564-6697
www.johnnyseeds.com

NICHOLS GARDEN NURSERY

1190 Old Salem Road NE
Albany, OR 97321
Phone: (800) 422-3985
www.nicholsgardennursery.com

PARK SEED CO.

1 Parkton Avenue
Greenwood, SC 29647
Phone: (800) 845-3369
www.parkseed.com

PINETREE GARDEN SEEDS

P.O. Box 300
New Gloucester, ME 04260
Phone: (207) 926-3400
www.superseeds.com

RENEE'S GARDEN

6060A Graham Hill Road
Felton, CA 95018
Phone: (888) 880-7228
www.reneesgarden.com

SEED SAVERS EXCHANGE

3094 North Winn Road
Decorah, IA 52101
Phone: (563) 382-5990
www.seedsavers.org

SEEDS OF CHANGE

P.O. Box 15700
Santa Fe, NM 87592
Phone: (888) 762-7333
www.seedsofchange.com

SEEDS TRUST

P.O. Box 4619
Ketchum, ID 43340
Phone: (208) 788-4363
www.seedstrust.com

SOUTHERN EXPOSURE SEED EXCHANGE

P.O. Box 460
Mineral, VA 23117
Phone: (540) 894-9480
www.southernexposure.com

STOKES SEED INC.

P.O. Box 548
Buffalo, NY 14240
Phone: (800) 396-9238
www.stokeseeds.com

STOKES SEED INC., CANADA

P.O. Box 10
Thorold, ON L2V 5E9
Canada
Phone: (800) 396-9238
www.stokeseeds.com

TERRITORIAL SEED COMPANY

P.O. Box 158
Cottage Grove, OR 97424
Phone: (800) 626-0866
www.territorialseed.com

Supplies

TOMATOFEST® HEIRLOOM TOMATO SEEDS

P.O. Box 628

Little River, CA 95456

www.tomatofest.com

TOMATO GROWERS SUPPLY CO.

P.O. Box 60015

Fort Myers, FL 33906

Phone: (888) 478-7333

www.tomatogrowers.com

TOTALLY TOMATOES

334 West Stroud Street

Randolph, WI 53956

Phone: (800) 345-5977

www.totallytomato.com

GARDENER'S SUPPLY CO.

128 Intervale Road

Burlington, VT 05401

Phone: (888) 833-1412

www.gardeners.com

GARDENS ALIVE!

5100 Schenley Place

Lawrenceburg, IN 47025

Phone: (513) 354-1482

www.gardensalive.com

HARMONY FARM SUPPLY & NURSERY

3244 Highway 116 North

Sebastopol, CA 95472

Phone: (707) 823-9125

www.harmonyfarm.com

PEACEFUL VALLEY FARM SUPPLY & GARDEN

P.O. Box 2209

Grass Valley, CA 95945

Phone: (888) 784-1722

www.groworganic.com

Resources

YOUR LOCAL COUNTY EXTENSION OFFICE

Every state has a "County Cooperative Agricultural Extension Service." Originally designed to help keep farmers informed, Extension Agents and their Master Gardener volunteers now offer advice and information to home gardeners as well. They are *the* experts on local conditions and peculiarities (like average frost dates and regional pest and disease pressures), and most offices offer inexpensive soil testing services through their parent Land Grant University. To find *your* local office, type the phrase "cooperative extension" plus the name of your state into any Internet search engine. The main page for your state's Extension Service will list all the local offices by county; find yours and give them a call.

Warning: You may be offered *extremely* non-organic advice with your soil test results or if you inquire about a pest or disease problem. If your state is so foolishly inclined, rely on them *only* for soil testing and issues of local climate and timing. No garden problem requires a chemical solution, and virtually all such "solutions" cause many more problems than they solve.

YOU BET YOUR GARDEN® ARCHIVES

At the end of every week's radio show, I deliver a detailed, heavily-researched answer to a specific garden and/or pest control question. All of these answers are archived alphabetically on the *You Bet Your Garden®* section of the Gardens Alive! website. This is where you'll find lots of detailed info on things like building raised beds and making and using compost. It's also where you'll find up-to-the-minute info on pest control topics—including details on pests that are just emerging as tomato threats as this revised edition goes to press, like the soon-to-be-notorious marmorated Asian stinkbug. To access these and hundreds of other organic articles, visit *https://www.gardensalive.com/category/you_bet_your_garden/a* and scroll through or search for your topic. (Or just type the words "You Bet Your Garden" into your favorite Internet search engine.) You can also listen to the show live, listen to old shows, and/or access the weekly podcast at the *You Bet Your Garden®* site *(www.youbetyourgarden.org)*.

Index

. . . .

Acquisition editor: Alan Giagnocavo
Plain White Press edition publisher: Julie Trelstad
Cover and layout designer: John Hoch
Layout: Chris Morrison
Interior photography: Gurney's Seed & Nursery Co., TomatoFest® Heirloom Tomato Seeds, David Cavagnaro, and John Kelsey; also see page 120
Illustrator: Signe Wilkinson
Editor: Katie Weeber (first edition); Colleen Dorsey (second edition)

Photo Credits

Unless otherwise noted, all photos are provided by Gurney's Seed & Nursery Company (*Gurneys.com*).

Special thanks to Donna Chiarelli Photography for the use of the author's photo appearing on the front cover and on page 7.

Special thanks to David Cavagnaro and TomatoFest® Heirloom Tomato Seeds (*www.tomatofest.com*) for the use of the marked photos appearing on the tomato chart on pages 24–33.

The images appearing on pages 72 and 92 have been used under the Creative Commons Attribution-ShareAlike 3.0 Unported (CC BY-SA 3.0) license. To learn more, visit *http://creativecommons.org/licenses*.

The following images are credited to Shutterstock.com and their respective creators: front cover: Sayanjo65; back cover second from top: CharMoment; 8: Valentina Razumova; 9: Hortimages; 16 top: Scott A . Burns; 16 bottom: Leo Zank; 17: Sebw; 36: Amelia Martin; 37: Gyvafoto; 38 top: Edgar Lee Espe; 38 bottom: Keith Homan; 39 top: spline_x; 39 middle: Anton Starikov; 39 bottom: Lifestyle discover; 42: Yala; 44: ChaiyonS021; 45: Judy M Darby; 47: Flower Studio; 50: Miriam Doerr Martin Frommherz; 51: Thomas Barrat; 52: Iakov Filimonov; 53: Koliadzynska Iryna; 57: KaliAntye; 82 top: Patricia Dulasi; 82 bottom: Mauro Rodrigues; 83: Doidam 10; 86: BMJ; 87: sangkhom sangkakam; 89: Nadeene; 94: LarisaL; 95: ThamKC; 96 top: M. L. Haen; 96 bottom: mountainpix; 97 top: Plant Pathology; 97 bottom: Bernd Schmidt; 98: Plant Pathology; 104: Mosab Bilto; 106: Zigzag Mountain Art; 107 top: Maddas; 107 bottom: Tatyana Abramovich; 108: concept w; 109: dragon_fang; 120: Diana Taliun.